Maria I. Diedrich, Theron D. Cook, Flip Lindo (Eds.)

Crossing Boundaries:
African American Inner City and European Migrant Youth

FORECAAST

(Forum for European Contributions
to African American Studies)

Volume 14

LIT

Maria I. Diedrich, Theron D. Cook, Flip Lindo (Eds.)

Crossing Boundaries:
African American Inner City
and European Migrant Youth

LIT

Umschlagbild: Claudio Scotoni, Firth of Forth

Die Herausgeber danken dem Collegium for African American Research (CAAR), der DFG, dem Fachbereich 9 der WWUM, der Village Foundation und der Westfälischen Wilhelms-Universität für die Unterstützung dieses Projekts.

Bibliographic information published by Die Deutsche Bibliothek
Die Deutsche Bibliothek lists this publication in the Deutsche Nationalbibliografie; detailed bibliographic data are available in the Internet at http://dnb.ddb.de.

ISBN 3-8258-7231-9

© **LIT VERLAG** Münster   2004
Grevener Str./Fresnostr. 2   48159 Münster
Tel. 0251-23 50 91   Fax 0251-23 19 72
e-Mail: lit@lit-verlag.de   http://www.lit-verlag.de

Distributed in North America by:

Transaction Publishers
New Brunswick (U.S.A.) and London (U.K.)

Transaction Publishers
Rutgers University
35 Berrue Circle
Piscataway, NJ 08854

Tel.: (732) 445-2280
Fax: (732) 445-3138
for orders (U. S. only):
toll free (888) 999-6778

Contents

Crossing Boundaries: Introductory Remarks   7
    Theron D. Cook, Maria I. Diedrich and Flip Lindo

Reflections on Transatlantic Replication of American Best Practice Models   21
    Theron D. Cook

Race, Rumor, and Public Policy: Urban Youth and the Framing of "Dangerousness"   27
    Gerard Fergerson

The African American Male Leadership Academy: A Case Study in the African American Experience   43
    Jacob U. Gordon

Contradictory Policies and Their Implementation: Ethiopian Youth in Transition   62
    Tamar Horowitz

Constructive and Constraining Masculinities: Masculinities and Racialization in Young Londoners   79
    Ann Phoenix

Youth Groups and the Politics of Time and Space   95
    Nora Räthzel

Dynamics of Integration and Segregation: Ethnic Minorities in Germany   115
    Birgit Rommelspacher

Social Exclusion and Cultures of Resistance Amongst Young Male Immigrant in the "New Sweden"   127
    Ove Sernhede

When Tradition Becomes Fashionable: The Case of Young Turkish Women in Belgium   144
    Christiane Timmerman

Responses to Migration in Italy: Social Integration and Representations of the "Immigrant"   163
    Mariangela Veikou

Contributors   183

Crossing Boundaries: Introductory Remarks
Theron D. Cook, Maria I. Diedrich and Flip Lindo

> We real cool. We
> Left school. We
>
> Lurk late. We
> Strike Straight. We
>
> Sing sin. We
> Thin gin. We
>
> Jazz June. We
> Die Soon.
>
> Gwendolyn Brooks[1]

Upon walking the streets and alleyways of any inner city anywhere in the United States you sooner or later come upon groups of black kids, gathering at a street corner, in a back alley, on a basketball court. Many of them will wear prison-style outfits – loose jeans without belts; sneakers unlaced; the basketball cap turned backwards. There is usually a boom box around, and rap music. And inevitably you will hear the N-word, tabooed between black and white, tossed back and forth between these kids in fierce defiance.

Upon entering a district housing migrants in any major European city you will encounter an almost identical scene – youngsters dressed in prison style, the boom box, rap. Only most of the kids are of a "white" or olive complexion: they are of Moroccan, Senegalese, Turkish, Russian, Serbian, Afghan, Chilean, Vietnamese, Yugoslavian, Polynesian background. And they call themselves "Wiggers," "white Niggers" or "Black albinos."

There can be no doubt that this imitation of what migrant youths in Europe perceive as a black lifestyle testifies to their fascination with an exotic "Other," with a romanticized black inner city youth culture as it is transmitted for an international audience via MTV, internet and other mass communication media. Yet, as Ove

---

[1] Blacks, by Gwendolyn Brooks was featured with the permission of Brooks Permissions and Third World Press.

Sernhede's work documents, it is so much more than just a mindless fashion statement. Wearing prison garb, using the rap lingo and moves, embracing the African American street kid as a model also mirrors an awareness in these youngsters of the precarious status to which the European communities that have become their reluctant homes away from home have relegated them.

It is expressive of life without perspective at the periphery, of unchanneled anger, of an existence defined by that pattern of poverty which Pierre Bourdieu has identified as "modern misery"; it is a response, finally, to overwhelming public representations that insist on portraying these adolescent immigrants as essentially different, inassimilable, unwanted. Indeed, viewed as a threat to the community's social and economic stability, as leeches depleting the nation's financial resources, and finally, as people without a future.

It also testifies to these youngsters' need for community, to their creative resources, to their *joie de vivre*, to the power that is in them while fostering both, new transnational alliances and gang cultures. Adopting a "Wigger" identity and embracing "blackness" as a state of mind is a political statement that establishes a link between those black Americans who were left behind in the inner city by the Civil Rights Movement and those youths in European cities of migrant background who are not allowed to belong. It is a move that forces us to acknowledge that today's mass migration confronts us with new notions of race, with new racialized discourses and practices, with new forms of racism – the French sociologist Etienne Balibar speaks of "racism without race."

In social theory, the non-existence of "race" as an empirical category, and its status as a social, ideological and – formerly – scientific construct is by now a widely accepted idea. We speak about the "racialization" of ethnic groups whenever social, economic, cultural or personal differences are defined as inherited or biological features. The public discourse in the United States and western Europe may embrace and affirm anti-racist norms as politically correct, but despite the anti-racist pose that has been widely adopted within contemporary pluralistic societies, the differentiation and exclusion of ethnic minority or immigrant groups on the basis of other criteria and assumptions than those of "racial" difference or even inferiority has been continued and legitimated in more subtle, sophisticated ways. Hence, race continues to matter.

Names given to forms of racism vary according to the national political, social and cultural context in which they are manifested. Specifically, in the 1980s scholars in the U.S. identified "new" expressions of racism as negative attitudes towards out-groups that were increasingly justified by the minority groups' non-compliance to in-group norms and values. Similarly, in a European discourse on "race" relations since then, the justifications for immigration control and the regulation of ethnic relations were no longer based on explicit assumptions about racial inferiority but on arguments about the cultural difference and incompatibility of ethnic minorities. Faced with the introduction of these essentializing concepts both in the United States and Europe, and confronted with the prevalence of more subtle contemporary forms of racism, inner city and migrant youth, by embracing blackness as a state of mind, articulate their everyday experience that race and racism are not solely the intellectual property of right-wing extremism. Race and racism are routines of perception that find vent in attitudes reproduced through everyday interaction, and they are perpetuated in popular dispositions which express beliefs in cultural incompatibility.

Nobody in the field of international migration studies would ever doubt the legitimacy and usefulness of comparing American and European patterns of migration. What has never been attempted, however, is placing the study of American inner city – and thus a native though marginalized American population – next to research on migrant youths in Western Europe. What is the logic and objective of bringing together these two groups, whose historical experiences, cultural backgrounds, and future perspectives seem to be defined in terms of difference rather than commonality?

It was the "Wigger" metaphor, with its implications of a trans-national youth response to uprootedness and racialized exclusion that inspired the Collegium for African American Research (CAAR) to invite African American scholars and NGOs working among American inner city black youngsters and European and Israeli migration scholars to initiate a research project called "Crossing Boundaries." This project takes a trans-cultural and trans-national approach, and it compares the situation of young African Americans in US-American inner cities and of migrant youths in major Old World cities.

The focus of this research project is the inner city and migrant communities themselves, and the transformational resources they contain and represent. This approach contrasts with the traditional analysis of strategies which the majoritarian or "host" communities developed to further or impede the integration of these migrant/inner city youth. This shift of paradigm is expressive of our conviction that scholarship needs to identify and unearth those rich – though often dormant – resources that lie <u>within</u> the migrant/inner city communities; to locate activities that tap the creative potential available <u>within</u> specific cultures; and to investigate and critique the institutionalized majoritarian responses to these activities. Ideal outcomes of our work will positively impact migrant communities through trans-national best practice replication, influence Old World national migrant and New World inner city policies, and further advance applied research to address grassroots migrant concerns.

European studies abound on the problems of vulnerable migrant youth. Yet, it remains relatively under-explored how people and institutions <u>within</u> the various migrant communities think about, and deal with the deplorable situation and often problematic behavior of a sizeable part of their youth. Indeed, there is scant information on the ideas and strategies these youth have developed to counteract their problems.

The focus of traditional migration research is overwhelmingly upon the apparent danger that youth groups with immigrant background represent for the safety and cohesion of the society at large. This research concentrates almost exclusively on the failure, the reluctance, or the inability of immigrant families to keep their children in hand. Further, it goes on to condemn the lack of effective institutions and checks in the community to contain, nay, neutralize the danger that many see embodied in these children – many of whom are so conspicuously present in the city streets ridden and rife with social problems.

While in public discourse on migration – especially in sensationalizing media representations – "danger" is specific to certain immigrant youth, the "Crossing Boundaries" project analyses the phenomenon as a more complex, structural one. This approach is designed to advance learning in the circumstances and reasons for an alleged new racism as it manifests itself through the differential opportunities, treatment and stereotyping of immigrant youth groups in European cities, and juxtaposes these findings with research on black kids in the American inner city.

Although research in inner-minority activities is still scarce, there is growing evidence that in most European immigration countries migrant community-based initiatives are being designed to ameliorate the situation of young people at risk. Most of this research on migrant community activities and institutions focuses on religious and/or political organizations that were usually created by first generation migrants. These activities often also define objectives that relate to their children, e.g., their religious or language education.

More recently, in several European countries initiatives have sprung up among fathers – themselves children of immigrants, but often born and partly raised in the community of orientation – to patrol the streets of their neighborhood, to keep in touch with their kids and to detain them from indulging in risk behavior. Another important migrant-community initiative is the formation of alternative media that targets immigrant youth in large cities. In Italy for example, where immigration and cultural diversity within the larger national community are far more recent phenomena than in the traditional immigration countries of northern Europe, there are newspapers distributed by and for the immigrants, written in part by immigrants, to promote the general social education within the newly shaped multicultural society.

One concept that is relevant for any analysis of black inner city and/or migrant community activities is that of social capital. Social capital as defined by Bourdieu, Portes and others refers to both, the value inherent to social relationships between people and to the capacity of individuals to command scarce resources by virtue of their membership in networks or broader social structures. It thus relates not only to the resources themselves but to the individual's ability to mobilize them on demand. Social capital, and social networks in particular, consequently reduce the costs and risks of migration by enhancing the chances of getting a good job in the receiving society or of finding an apartment; social capital plays a defining role in the process of creating an immigrant niche. Moreover, it plays a defining role in shaping the destiny of individual migrant youth.

Recent scholarship has shown that the use of social capital and the constitution of social networks can vary considerably from one immigrant group to another. Since access to socio-economic resources is necessarily influenced decisively by the policies of the host society, it is to be expected that variations in the use of social capital is not only one aspect that distinguishes different groups of immigrants but also members of the same ethnic group in different host societies. From this observation it follows that the acquisition and the utilization of social capital cannot be explained by simply focusing on ethnic group-membership alone. Instead, it is crucial to take the socio-economic and politico-legal context as unavoidably significant into account. These findings then need to be correlated with specific events where social capital is gained and activated, e.g., political engagement.

Clearly, migration is rapidly and dramatically changing the face of Europe. Since World War II, but especially in the past two decades, the politically disowned, the persecuted, the impoverished and the uprooted from all over the world have fled to Europe in their struggle for survival, transforming the continent. None of the European receiver countries have been gracious hosts, while each and every one balked at the merest suggestion that these new Ethiopian, Afghan, Turkish, Ugandan, Moroccan, Vietnamese or Russian neighbors – to list only a few – could be fellow citizens, and a part of the new and future Europe. Those seeking shelter encountered segregation, discrimination and violence; they faced hostile administrations, exclusivist legislation, social ostracism, and hate crime. Xenophobia and blatant racism were rekindled. Sadly, each European country boasts its own LePen; and nowhere do the LePens lack disciples or ready ears.

The United States is per se a nation of immigrants. However, there is legitimate doubt whether this definition can and should be applied to the African American segment of its population. After all, they were involuntary pioneers to the New World-- violently kidnapped from their African homelands; a people in whose cosmology America as either dream or locale was non-existent; unwitting prisoners exposed to a terrifying Middle Passage with destiny unknown; an amalgam of individuals from different tribes sold as slaves in a land that contained no recognizable landmarks.

Contemporary U.S. scholarship, and especially expert social scientists agree that most of the symptoms of social dislocation and pathology – violence, HIV infections, drug addiction, crime, suicide, teenage pregnancy – that characterize the situation of African American youth in U.S. inner city neighborhoods today have their historical roots in the institution of slavery and its apartheid aftermath. Racial slavery, as it developed in its specific form in the North American colonies and the young United States, not only deprived people of African descent of their personal freedom and exposed them to extreme forms of exploitation; by defining slaves as chattel the system also denied their status as human beings.

This relegation to a position outside of or below the human race had a devastating impact on the status of African Americans in American society even after the abolition of slavery. In fact, racist assumptions developed under the Peculiar Institution were joined to the "findings" of a scientific racism that dominated the American discourse on race during the second half of the nineteenth century. As a result, for more than a century these arguments were used to justify the exclusion of African Americans from political participation, their social and economic segregation and political discrimination. Indeed, these views culminated in American society routinely denouncing them as either infantile Sambos or potential rapists. To this day, this racialized discourse is perpetuated subtly and not so subtly in U.S. mass media, as evidenced in the widespread representation of inner city African Americans as gang members, rapists, killers, and welfare recipients, i.e., as vermin posing a threat to the body politic. The fact that the vast majority of black individuals from an inner city environment hold jobs, acquire an education, and abstain from violence and drugs is conveniently ignored.

Among European immigration specialists it is often not realized that the African American population in the inner cities in the North, South and West of the United States – but of course also the vast black middle classes in the "better" parts of town – is a population of internal migrants and their descendants. Their migration experience is inextricably linked to their kidnapping from Africa, to the conditions to which they were subjected in the South, to the racially legitimated barriers that were put up to prevent them from migrating to the North, and to the racialized discrimination they suffered when they were allowed to settle in the cities.

When, in the course of the nineteenth century, the predominantly European immigrants came to the United States and settled in New York, they found a city with an almost invisible black population and a stagnating black internal migrant population. The now large African American population in the American cities thus can be considered as a more recent internal immigrant population than the mostly European immigrants from the nineteenth century.

In the United States, the inner city found itself with a population that did not profit from the liberating impact of the Civil Rights Movement and legislation. This was a population that was left behind and forgotten when their more successful Sisters and Brothers moved to safer and more respectable segments of the city. This phenomenon has become a metaphor for America's catastrophic failure in taking on the issues of race that face the nation. Public discourse defines the inner city as a realm of crime, stagnation, disease, hopelessness and racial incompatibility, with its youth as a gang culture.

Similarly, in Europe, major cities like Rome, Marseille, Berlin, Stockholm, Paris, London, Frankfurt and Amsterdam have housing projects for the migrant population that are situated on the periphery. Socio-economic and political policies have perverted these projects into sites of inbred violence and chronic unemployment; into problem zones where traditional social institutions like family, school and church/mosque are deteriorating. European mass media revel in narratives of fierce wars between gangs of migrant youths and gangs of "natives," battles that are motivated by extreme forms of nationalism, xenophobia, and racial hatred.

Both migrant populations – today's migrants from all over the world in European cities and inner city African Americans – thus suffer from negative, racialized stereotyping by sectors of the indigenous or Euro-American population and their institutions. These peripheral populations are victims of drastic structural changes in Europe and the United States. The African American community as well as their European migrant counterparts contain many families suffering social dislocation that can in large measure be accounted for by the immigration process.

And, perhaps even more important to the "Crossing Boundaries" objective, another phenomenon is clear: within the African American populations in the inner cities and within the migrant communities of European cities, one can identify numerous effective grassroots initiatives, deeply embedded in these diverse communities, that work to ameliorate the position of youth at risk. These hopeful and proven initiatives provide a beacon for governments, academics, and the media looking for viable ways to address the increasing and multiple issues surrounding the necessary integration of migrants and their descendants into societies around the world.

Crossing Boundaries: Introductory Remarks

The articles assembled in this volume reflect a first attempt to establish a trans-Atlantic and trans-cultural research perspective via an exchange based on the individual project participant's work in progress.

Theron D. Cook's article, "Reflections on Transnational Replication of American Best Practice Models," explores the many different programmatic and planning aspects that policy makers, foundation executives, and academics must take into account when contemplating adopting American best practices programs and models abroad. Cook discusses myriad areas of planning and organizational requirements that are needed to ensure that any American model being considered for replication has a better than good chance of surviving past its first wave of funding, to meet its mission, and to achieve qualitative and quantitative outcomes in its new environment. Specific areas of analysis include: leadership, funding, program content, unintended consequences, and turf issues. Cook's broad-brush approach to these issues is intended to set the parameters for greater discussion and more detailed analysis for those individuals with the means and will to take the best of what the United States has to offer vis-à-vis best and promising practices, and adopt them abroad.

Gerard Fergerson's "Race, Rumor, and Public Policy: Urban Youth and the Framing of 'Dangerousness'" analyzes media and policy discourse as it relates to the framing of black youth criminality in urban environments. The author contends that perceptions of race and "dangerousness" for black youth reflect racist ideas about predisposition to criminality that impact options for public intervention in cities. Arguing that public policy is often premised on rumors and tales, as opposed to social science, Fergerson shows that fatalistic representations of black urban youth are encoded in policy and media narratives which stereotype urban environments and result in discriminatory policies reflecting a range of cultural, class, race, and gender biases. Contrary to popular and policy discourses centered on tales of escalating urban youth violence, Fergerson offers a historical contextualization of contemporary youth development and juvenile justice policy. At bottom, his analysis advances a call to invoke more effectively narrative and cultural analysis into discussions of public policy.

In "The African-American Male Leadership Academy: A Case Study in the African American experience" Jacob U. Gordon from the University of Kansas claims that no serious academic endeavor can deny the impact of the trans-Atlantic slave trade and slavery as well as migration on the American people. Scholars of plantation slavery have documented the global impact of these events, e.g., the "separate but equal" doctrine resulting from the 1896 Supreme Court decision in the case of *Plessy v. Ferguson*, as a major contributor to the current status of African Americans. In addition, the black exodus from the antebellum South to northern industrial urban communities in the 1870s only provided a temporary solution to the black exclusion. Thus, Gordon contends, the plight of African American men and their families require special attention.

Gordon's paper examines the African-American Male Leadership Academy as a replicable demonstration model. The program was designed to ameliorate the conditions of the African American male in four cities: Topeka, Kansas; Wichita, Kansas; Kansas City, Kansas; and Kansas City, Missouri. The basic logic evaluation model was used to document program outcomes and impact.

The integration of Ethiopian immigrant youth, which Tamar Horowitz from the Ben Gurion University in Israel delineates in "Contradictory Policies and their Implementation: Ethiopian Youth in Transition," is a story full of contradictions. She explores the general philosophy of Israeli immigration policy to encourage the immigrants to preserve their identity, but in reality they were under constant pressure to assimilate into Israeli society. The Israeli government claimed to respect their traditions while deligitimizing their religious leaders.

The order of the day was not to be patronizing, but the absorption centers in which the immigrants originally stayed represented a patronizing attitude and dependence. The policy was to avoid having large numbers of Ethiopian students in the same schools; still, many of them ended up in homogeneous Ethiopian schools. Affirmation action was employed, yet many people could not get into universities because they did not have matriculation certificates. While the government policy was considered free of racism, racism permeated Israeli society at large, Horowitz argues. These contradictory policies and practices explain why the identity construction of young Ethiopians in Israel was and continues to be so complicated.

In "Constructive and Constraining Masculinities: Masculinities and Racialization in Young Londoners" Ann Phoenix from the Open University in Milton Keynes, England addresses the contradictions between positive features of "multicultures" such as increases in friendships and relationships across ethnicized groups as well as syncretic style and "multi-racisms", characterized by racist attacks and informal segregation. She identifies some of these contradictions as they relate to British young people. In particular, she focuses on the racialized complexity and contradictions produced in the educational context and on the contradictions faced and produced for young black men as they negotiate masculinities at school.

The paper contends that British society is marked by contradictions between multi-ethnicity and multi-racisms – contradictions that are evident within the education system, both in terms of the qualifications children obtain and the everyday practices common in schools. The racialization of popular masculinities in schools apparently places them out of the reach of white boys and particularly Asian boys while defining black boys outside "normality" and so opening them to treatment as "Other" and "too hard" by teachers and white boys.

Phoenix argues that racialization makes contestation about masculinities and differential positioning an important aspect of boys' subjectivities and contributes to anxieties and contradictions for boys. The paper shows that, in order to understand the challenges inherent in achieving racialized and gendered equality in schools, one needs to consider the reasons why boys are not entirely free to choose to behave in ways likely to improve their future educational attainment. These reasons include boys' concern to manage the present rather than the future in the context of complicated, multiple positioning that requires them to compete with each other in terms of toughness and style if they are to be accepted as properly masculine.

"Youth Groups and the Politics of Time and Space" is based on a three-year study of young people in a large German town. Nora Räthzel from Umea University in Sweden looks at the way in which members of two youth groups present themselves and their group in terms of the places they occupy and to the traditions they relate. The stage of transition from adolescence to adulthood, usually seen as a time in which young people fluctuate between different places and time-structures, invokes desires of unchangeable places and circular time structures in the young group members. The paper explains these desires through an analysis of the spatial and political context in which these young people of migrant background live. As they are positioned as "foreigners" in a society that rejects them as legitimate members, holding on to a place in which diversity is seen as an asset seems the only way to preserve a sense of belonging and self-respect. However, Räthzel contends that such active appropriation of a place can also be seen as reproducing and accepting the relegation to only one place.

Birgit Rommelspacher's article on "Dynamics of Integration and Segregation: Ethnic Minorities in Germany" shows that the strategies for integration and segregation that were adopted by different immigrant countries are, aside from the expressed economic and political interests, largely a product of their self-images with respect to heterogeneity and equality. Despite a century-long history of emigration and immigration, the political culture in Germany has mainly been shaped by a vision of a closed and homogeneous society, i.e., by visions that result primarily from the difficult process of German nation building.

The notion of assimilation is quite strong, and immigrants are judged by the extent to which they identify with German culture. This also played a decisive role during German unification, whereby the West Germans usurped the right to define what is supposed to be "genuinely" German. By means of this symbolic power it is determined who has access to economic resources and political power in society. This is seen in economic, social, political and cultural dimensions of segregation that divide societies along ethnic lines. Racially motivated violence is the most vociferous expression of these segregationist tendencies. To fight these tendencies suggests not only combating racism and violence; it also necessitates a transformation in the German self-image in terms of forging a more pluralistic, democratic and egalitarian society.

Ove Sernhede's "Social Exclusion and Cultures of Resistance amongst Young Male Immigrants in 'The New Sweden'" deals with young, male immigrants engaged in hip hop culture in contemporary Sweden. The currents of migration, processes of marginalization and patterns of segregation that have profoundly transformed Sweden during the 1990s, tend to make non-Western immigration synonymous with social exclusion. The focus of the article is on how a particular group of young males in one of the immigrant dense suburbs of Gothenburg use hip hop culture as a way to build a multi-ethnic youth community. Hip hop is also considered as a way to get out in public and fight racism and social injustice. "The microphones is our shoot guns, the words are our bullets".

Research in the tradition of cultural studies has shown that cultures developed by the young often make visible antagonisms and conflicts that exist below the surface of society. The immigrant youth grow up in a society where ethnic boundaries are inflicted and where social inequality is transformed into and explained as cultural differences. Sernhede contends that the social and cultural logic at work under these conditions leads to a situation in which young people's sub-cultural resistance also adopts ethnified forms of appearance. The poses, attitudes and jargons of the Northern American ghetto culture tend to offer an exclusive counter-identity – for "Blackheads" only.

Turkish immigrants who settle in Belgium are confronted with a way of life that differs in many respects from the one they were accustomed to in their native country, Christine Timmerman from the University of Antwerp, Belgium argues in "When Tradition Becomes Fashionable: The Case of Young Turkish Women in Belgium." Moreover, their children and grandchildren – although they are raised and socialized in western society – remain closely connected with Turkey and indeed define themselves firmly as Turks. Ethno-nationalism among Turkish immigrants is undoubtedly fuelled by the strong patriotism, both secular and religious, that one encounters in Turkey itself. On the other hand, the ways in which this nationalistic heritage is interpreted is influenced strongly by the concrete reality of the context of immigration. Timmerman's paper focuses on expressions of this dynamic among young Turkish women living in Belgium.

Mariagela Veikou's "Responses to Migration in Italy: Representation of the 'Immigrant' and Immigrant Integration" is based on research conducted during 2000-1 in Florence, Italy in the context of an international project, funded by the European Commission. This project concentrated on making sense of Italy, as well as three other European countries – Germany, UK and Greece – as an immigrant receiving society. Data from interview texts gathered during that period are analyzed, to examine and reflect on the representation of immigrants in Italian society, as revealed in the daily practice of two agencies involved with the implementation of immigration law provisions, a Provincial Foreigners' Office of the Police Headquarters and an Accommodation Centre. The aim was to study the synchronic aspects of culture manifested in talk, values, beliefs of the employees and clients therein. Against this knowledge, Veikou reveals various themes in the representation of immigrants in this framework of employee/agent versus client/immigrant context of relation.

Collectively, these articles render a thorough understanding of the intricacies yet commonality of the migrant experience in host countries. Through a strong analysis of these commonalities the Crossing Boundaries group seeks a better understanding on how best to address the myriad socio-economic and political-legal challenges that migrants face and their host countries must confront. With the world shrinking daily, it behooves us all to find more effective and life-affirming ways of living together as opposed to the traditional approach of marginalizing and hence, criminalizing those who do not look like us.

Reflections on Transatlantic Replication of American Best Practice Models

Theron D. Cook

As international policy makers, foundations, academics and community leaders ponder how best to export American best and promising practice models, one thing is clear. While replication as an end is laudable, the means to that end is fraught with barriers, challenges and prerequisites. In essence, myriad issues have to be considered strategically and planned for before implementation of the replication process in order to achieve the desired outcome. Indeed, the following areas of consideration have to be analyzed and properly vented during the planning stage before starting any replication efforts: leadership, funding, program content, unintended consequences, and turf issues. While seemingly daunting in the number of issues that need to be broached, once accomplished in a systematic fashion, successful transnational replication is highly achievable.

Leadership

Leadership is the first major consideration that must be made to ensure success in the replication effort. Further, different forms of leadership have to be well thought-out at several crucial levels: individual, board and community. Exceptional leadership at the executive director level marks most successful programs. For American community-based, grassroots and nonprofit organizations, the leader is usually the charismatic founder or his/her successor whose force of personality, contacts, and leadership qualities are unique, but effectively achieves the mission of the organization. Furthermore, he/she is usually surrounded – and to a fair degree – guided by an involved board of directors who have bought into the mission and through their volunteered time, provides essential policy and organizational leadership to the agency. Finally, local support in the guise of one or several officials, councilmen or other municipal leaders is crucial. While many times their only tangible support comes in the form of an occasional letter of support for some external funding stream, their participation is important and invaluable when it comes to protecting existing funding. They can also provide insights and actual grants to the organization, if they are properly brought into the process, once that organization has gained enough of a "track record" not to merit continued political distance.

Community leadership comes in the form of acceptance by the local community of the mission and functions of the organization. Acceptance is key as the Not In My Backyard (NIMBY) phenomenon has been the brake on American domestic replication efforts and poses a significant challenge for any international replication attempts. It is at these times where the community leader can play an invaluable role in thwarting local attempts at preventing the model from being established. Their knowledge of and advocacy for the program becomes key to its eventual establishment.

When considering transnational replications, all of the above-mentioned areas have to be explored thoroughly. Specifically, the chief executive chosen to head up the new project in all probability will not have the exact same qualities as the original, but he/she must possess enough of them to successfully create the model anew. Those leadership qualities must contain the ability to understand not only the model, but to be able to tailor it to its new and necessarily different dynamics. Indeed, success or failure will be contingent on that individual's talent at organizational leadership. Hence, one must scrutinize and settle these leadership issues before replicating internationally.

Funding

Perhaps the single most ongoing challenge of any nonprofit, funding is the lifeblood of a replicated model. Moreover, one cannot overstate sustained funding as a necessity. For successful replication to occur, various funding streams have to be identified prior to and after the initial underwriting has been secured. While limited initially by the parameters, guidelines and dictates of the "first wave" funder, the leadership of the replicated model has to implement successfully a thoroughly thought-out and prepared fund development plan to acquire additional and sustained fundings —preferably from local, national and private sources.

This strategic funding plan should be a part of the initial application for funds, as many, if not all, funders want to know where other monies are being sought. If it is not attached to the initial application, one such plan should be developed with the assistance of external experts, through either a consultant or an agency that specializes in developing such plans. The goal is to research, find, and secure these funds as quickly as possible. This activity necessarily poses challenges for the operations of the fledgling organization as its mission is not to raise money, but to meet and address identified social needs.

Hence, the replicated models initial hires must include development professionals who can assist leadership in securing needed operational capital. Leadership has to be sophisticated enough to be able to balance operational needs with fund development necessities. Addressing this ever-present requirement of raising money, leadership has to be prepared to secure large and long-term funding to ensure future survivability. Thus, the replicated model's long-term survival is determined by targeted, strategic short and long-term fund development activities by its leadership. As such, a strategic fund development plan should be completed within the first or second quarter of operations, if it is not a part of the original replication plan.

Program Content

To be considered for replicating abroad, an American model's program content has already been ascertained to have worth. Yet, its value was necessarily judged within an American context with local parameters and dynamics. To fully determine whether the model's replicability abroad is viable, one has to consider all aspects of the program content, scrutinizing its strengths and weaknesses. Moreover, an honest analysis has to occur to determine whether a program's operational strengths – when taken out of its home context – can still be strengths or become liabilities abroad. In addition, if these liabilities were to become real, can those operational strengths be tweaked or transformed in an international context and still maintain their original integrity and effectiveness?

For example, consider an intervention program that is targeted to be replicated and its program's core component is a rite of passage program that relies on strong Christian teachings of morality, ethics and non-violence. The latter is important as the youth involved are violence prone and have had small brushes with the law. Outcomes desired from the program include violence reduction, increased school attendance, decreased brushes with law enforcement, and higher academic achievement. Due to its effectiveness, this model is being considered for replication in an inner city neighborhood in St. Denis, a suburb of Paris. Yet, a major concern arises when it becomes clear that the new-targeted clientele are going to be young Muslim boys of Northern African extraction.

Hence, hard questions have to be asked as to whether or not the Christian-based curriculum – once necessarily changed – can be as effective in a Muslim context. Further, after adjusting the model to meet the new demographic realities, should the outcomes necessarily have to change – especially since it was those initial outcomes and the program's effectiveness that originally made the model a candidate for replication? Other questions to be considered include: Is the program's content transferable? Is the program's success only due to a charismatic leader, or is it the curriculum? Does the program's strengths allow them to be changed without losing their intrinsic efficacy? These queries are at the core of any professional analysis to determine the likelihood of successful replication efforts.

Unintended Consequences

In the 1940s in a small Iowa town, there was a major explosion in the raccoon population. It seemed everywhere one turned, raccoons were visible: on people's porches, in their gardens, and in their garbage bins. They were a real nuisance, and some town elders considered them a public health menace. Hence, the town fathers got together and devised a plan to eradicate the raccoons. It worked, but before they could finish congratulating themselves, they realized that they now had a frog problem that was worse than the raccoon problem. They did not know that the reasons why there were so many raccoons was the last three years of unseasonable rain had produced an overabundance of frogs – which they never saw because the raccoons were effective in keeping them under control.

People, like animals, are inextricably tied to a social network. As a result, any good replication effort has to predict accurately what will happen when the program achieves its short-term goals and objectives. Moreover, is the model and the community it serves going to be prepared for the changes that are going to necessarily occur? For example, consider a Miami, Florida-based drug intervention and prevention model that is successfully implemented in a West African inner city targeting teenage boys who sell heroin. After six months of intensive interventions on the part of the replicated program, the numbers of boys selling drugs dramatically decreased. Due to the marked drop in income in that local community, girls are now being forced or "firmly encouraged" into prostitution by their destitute families. Boys who were once selling are now using, while crime is steadily increasing, as those newfound drug addicts need to support their newfound addictions. These are all unintended consequences because of an initial success achieved by the program. Such cause-effect scenarios have to be played out and anticipated by the leadership of the program that is being replicated before program implementation.

Turf Issues
Human beings, being who they are, have a tendency to view foreigners with suspicion and mistrust. When organizations – especially nonprofits – encounter another nonprofit, the initial response often is not one of collaboration, but of fear that the new organization will encroach on its territory or "catchment area" and, more importantly, siphon much needed funding away from its already overstretched budget. When considering putting a nonprofit model abroad, it is imperative that efforts are made to mitigate local tendencies to view the incoming program with suspicion if not outright hostility. Implicit in any placement of a program to solve a local problem is that the local community cannot do it alone: they need outside help.

Moreover, when that outside help is an American model, some local hostility is to be anticipated. Managing and negotiating that hostility will be the assignment of the local director and his/her staff. However, efforts can be made prior to program implementation to minimize negative feelings. These efforts should include meetings with community leaders and potential organizational rivals, hopefully in the presence of some political representation. Their presence serves two important purposes: 1) legitimizes the project; and 2) serves notice that if anything negative should happen to it through local shenanigans, there will be costs to pay.

Further efforts might include establishing as quickly as possible memoranda of understanding with potential rivals for referral purposes and to create the "win-win" scenarios needed to reduce jealousies and territoriality. These semi-contracts will be a result of establishing a working relationship with the rival executive directors and reducing their anxieties. It is the effectiveness of these "local politics" on the street level that will determine the long-term relationship that the replicated model will have with the community it seeks to serve and the efficacy of its programmatic outcomes.

Conclusion

Replication of American best and promising practices as evidenced above is a complicated and somewhat daunting task. Yet, when approached systematically – at the planning stage – with the intent of covering all potential problems and pitfalls, successful replications are not only possible, but also highly feasible. We have many examples of success, but sadly more examples of failures. In these times of increased social needs, decreased public policy money, and tighter philanthropic purse strings, international program replication makes great sense. With the existence of highly evaluated American models with already proven programmatic effectiveness, there is little need to reinvent the wheel to address similar problems abroad. However, to replicate cost-effectively and to ensure long-term sustainability, strategic planning and implementation covering these vital areas – leadership, funding, program content, unintended consequences, and turf issues – is necessary. Without such planning, any such replication efforts will be akin to throwing good seed on hard ground with hungry birds waiting to devour them.

Race, Rumor, and Public Policy: Urban Youth and the Framing of "Dangerousness"

Gerard Fergerson

On April 20, 2002, the national news in the United States highlighted the experience of a group of high school students in the town of Littleton, Colorado (Rimer 2002). The occasion marked the third anniversary of the school shooting in that town, where 14 students and a teacher were killed by two white male students (Kenworthy 1999). Shocked as the country was by the events of April 1999, Littleton joined a list of other towns and small cities, including Jonesboro, Arkansas (March 24, 1998) and West Paducah, Kentucky (December 1, 1997), where school shootings resulting in homicides made the national news. Indeed, a month to the day after Littleton, six students were injured in a shooting in the small town of Conyers, Georgia (Finn 2002; Bragg 1998).

Media representations of school shootings and the environments in which they occur are important for several reasons. For many contemporary researchers and policy makers, they represent the "problem of youth violence" in the United States. For this analysis, however, I would like to focus on the inscription of cultural, class, gender and racial biases that are reflected in policy and popular narratives about youth violence. These narratives represent powerful symbols in informal and formal policy processes, where options for public intervention are commonly based on rumor and fatalistic narratives about youth in urban environments. I also contend that these fatalistic and deterministic ideas about urban youth – and the environments that they inhabit – inscribe biases, even as specific and direct references to race, gender, class, geography, and culture are erased.

The representation of the shootings in Littleton, Colorado was especially stark in its messages about crime and geography, as news outlets fueled popular and policy narratives that these seemingly unexpected school shootings had occurred among "good" kids from "good places" (Rimer 2002). Shortly after the shootings in Littleton, for example, *The New York Times* lamented that this incident would enable the suburban community with "high S.A.T. scores" to "understand the real world."

Together with its readership the paper marveled at the increasing specter of violence in predominantly white and "stable" middle-class America. In addition to its focus on the apparent surprise about white juvenile delinquency as revealed through school shootings in the small Colorado town, the *Times* article is noteworthy for its linking of a suburban and rural geography with youth safety. Of course, this characterization ignores the evidence pointing to escalating youth violence, particularly gun violence, in predominately white suburban and rural counties (Anderson *et al.* 2001). And, even though the coverage of Columbine shared a similar experience from fatal school shootings in "mostly white, largely blue-collar college town" of Jonesboro, Arkansas, the metric of class has assured that the mostly white and upper middle class Littleton would be recognized in highly visible commemorations (Connolly 2000; Bragg 1998). Still, the erasure of black youth victimization and the framing of urban youth as "super-predators" endures through encoded messages about the social geography of youth violence in Columbine, Littleton, and elsewhere (Finn 2002; Becker 2001; US DHHS 2001).

In addition to an analysis of how representations of black youth criminality are encoded in narratives of urban youth violence, the objective of this article is to analyze the ways in which policy rumors and tales, as well as media representations of urban youth, ignore definitive social research data outlining historical and contemporary declines in youth violence (BRC 2001; Mendel 2001). This is also having an impact on national and local policy. Appealing to popular perceptions that youth violence is rising, some policy officials and researchers argue that investments in community-based youth development programs, diversion programs at the "front door", and other ameliorative measures to prevent youth from entering the juvenile justice system are not having an impact. This discussion will advance a counter narrative through analysis of data from Washington, D.C. and other cities, where precipitous declines in youth violence present evidence which undermines popular perceptions that youth violence is rising and that youth violence constitutes an overwhelming percentage of violent crime in urban environments. It is my hope that an analysis of these representations and policy impacts will draw more attention to the unique characteristics of the increased incarceration and restrictive commitment of youth and the blurring of the historical distinction between the adult centered criminal and juvenile justice systems (Butts 2002; Griffin 1998).

Youth Violence: Myths and Reality

In spite of the well-documented and prominent national and local declines in youth violence and crime in urban areas over the past decade, rumor masquerading as social science continues to influence popular perception and public policy related to youth violence. Recent policy discourse has almost made youth violence synonymous with urban youth, as evidenced by the media fascination with Littleton and other media reports of (white) juvenile delinquency in suburban environments (Gilliam 2001; Dorfman and Schiraldi 2001). Many pundits and researchers do not even believe the empirical data from solid studies and reporting of public officials. The data, however, are unequivocal on two levels. First, school shootings by white youth and general delinquency occurs with frequency in mostly white suburban and rural settings.[1] And, second, youth violence and crime rates have declined in urban areas, even when increases have been reported in suburban areas (US DHHS 2001).

In Washington, D.C., for example, once dubbed "the murder capital of the world" in the 1980s and 1990s because of its high murder rate, youth crime and violence has fallen by forty percent (40%) since the recent peak years of 1993 and 1994 (BRC 2001). This has been a consistent and even decline. An independent Blue Ribbon Commission on Youth Safety and Juvenile Justice Reform in the city documented that violent deaths to teenagers in 1999 were a third of what they were in 1993. Juvenile homicides (committed by youth), which stood at 69 in 1990 and twelve in 1998, were down to five by 2001. Several community-based partners illustrated that between 1990 and 1998, the rate of homicides per 100,000 youth under 18 years of age in D.C. fell by eighty percent (80%).[2] This exceeded a national decline of fifty two percent (52%). Paralleling a decline in youth homicides over the same period, the Superior Court of the District of Columbia reported a uniform decline in Juvenile Cases for all causes, crimes against persons, and crimes against property (see Figure 1).

Even with the strong evidence that youth violence rates for person and property offenses have declined significantly since the mid 1990s, narratives and tales of youth violence and criminality in the media and recent public policy continue to represent urban youth as exceptionally dangerous and their living environments as predisposed to negative social behaviors (Puritz *et al.* 2000). These are foremost fatalistic and deterministic racialized and gendered tales, which depict "super-predators" from an "underclass" environment as murderers and rapists who would not and do not benefit from violence prevention or other state-sponsored ameliorative measures. Prison and harsh sentences are often viewed as the only policy prescription to counter trends in youth crime and black criminality in general (Davis 2002). As downward trends in youth homicide and other violent crimes in Washington, D.C. and other major American cities supply empirical data from the mid 1990s onward demonstrating the nature of these declines, cultural conservatives, such as William J. Bennett, John J. DiIulio, Jr., and John P. Walters would argue that "America is now home to thickening ranks of juvenile 'super-predators'." (Bennett *et al.* 1996).[3] And, despite the fact that DiIulio has since discredited his own term and acknowledged that he was wrong in his assertion that prevention does not work, these ideas survive in popular discourse and contribute to ineffective and discriminatory public policy (e.g., racial profiling, disinvestments in community-based prevention programs, waiving of confidentiality, etc.). In other words, tales of urban "super-predators" have eclipsed evaluations of community-based interventions highlighting gains in youth development, and contributed to public policy inaction being premised on rumor and tales.

Before proceeding to an analysis of how these deterministic tales have influenced public policy trends, let me also join political theorists Deborah Stone, Sanford Schram, Philip T. Neisser, and others who stress how important it is that policy researchers, advocates, and public officials aggressively apply narrative analysis to public policy processes (Stone 1997; Schram 1997). Writing in *Tales of the State*, Sanford Schram and Philip T. Neisser note that we must strive to show "how policy narrative is a particularly effective medium for reinscribing race, gender, or class identities in ways that have profound political consequences affecting how people both get to influence and are influenced by politics." Tales and rumor – even in the face of quantitative and qualitative data demonstrating otherwise – often determine our policy options. Again, he cautions us to "interrogate all policy-making activity for its narrativity and assess the consequences given the pervasiveness of particular tales."

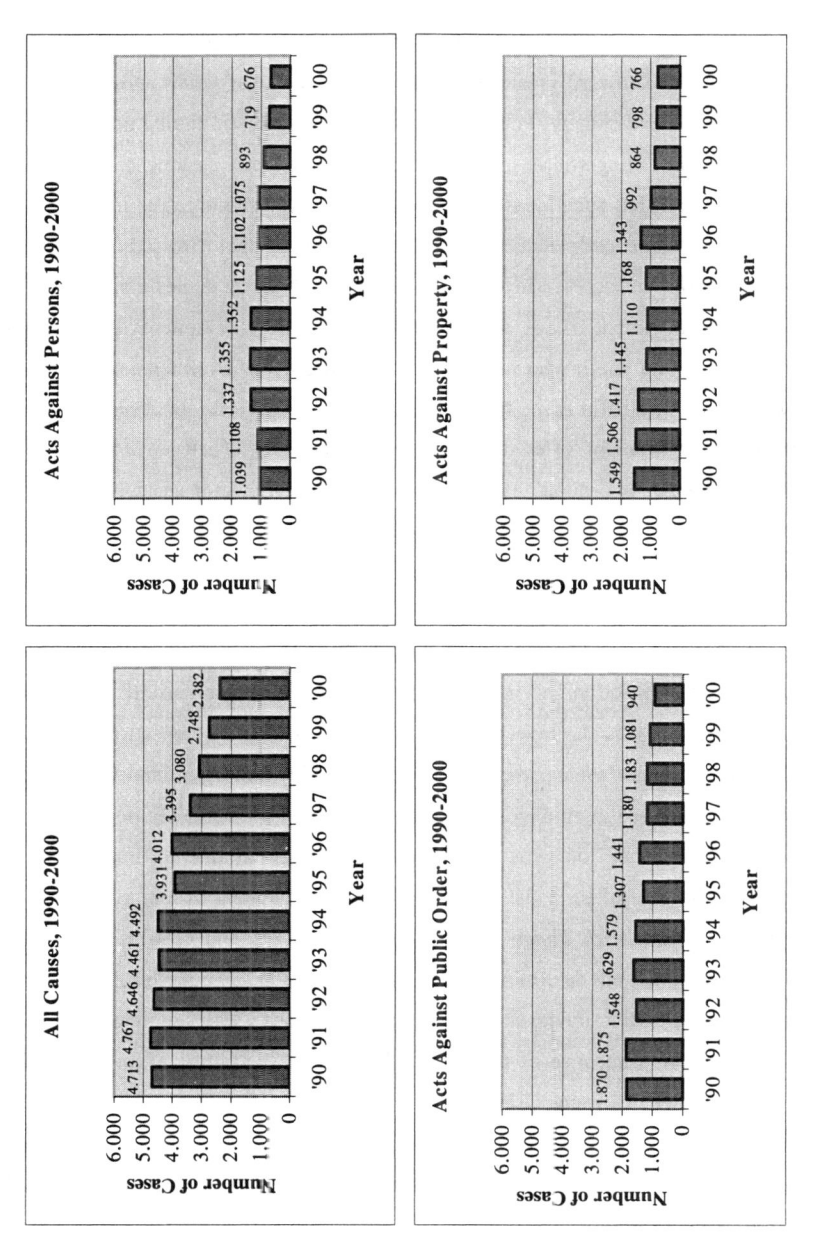

[Figure 1: Juvenile Cases Referred to D.C. Superior Court, 1990-2000]

The Anatomy of a Super-Predator: The Historical Context of the Culture Determinism in Contemporary Public Policy

The emergence of the "super-predator" thesis during the mid to late 1990s helped to solidify a trend toward greater calls for imprisonment of youth and disinvestment in urban youth development. Popular and scientific discourses linking perceptions of race to ideas about dangerousness and violence have existed as long as blacks lived on American soil, but such ideas in the 1990s would contribute to the institutionalization of federal, state, and local youth "justice" policies that stressed punishment over rehabilitation, an increase in waivers to adult court for juveniles convicted of violent and some nonviolent crimes, and a decline in support for community-based alternatives for children and youth who were found to be delinquent Dorfman and Schiraldi 2001; Demuro 1999; Griffin *et al.* 1998). I have written elsewhere about how this racial and cultural determinism offered stories of a racialized urban environment, i.e., the "underclass neighborhood" as the primarily immutable factor causing violence, crime, and drug problems (Fergerson 1997). Reductive scientific and cultural formulations have become increasingly encoded and hidden in media and policy narratives of the urban environment.

The super-predator thesis inscribes tales of urban minority males and females who are viewed as those largely responsible for school violence and other types of youth crime. The point is that oversimplifying narratives have influenced the reporting and naming of violent events, the formulation of policy strategies, and the evaluation of existing initiatives in an ongoing process of social stratification Butterfield 2000; Cole 1999). In the case of racial profiling in urban environments, police and judicial practices have resulted in the disproportionate confinement of minority youth. By late 1992, *The New York Times* – usually sedate on race and class issues – noted the problem of a nascent determinism in an editorial entitled "Young black Men": "There's nothing inherently criminal in young black men of the 1990s any more than there was in young immigrant men of the 1890s." Reminding the public of an earlier historical context in which young Irish and Italian immigrant males were stereotyped and "racially profiled" by the state in cities such as Boston and New York, the editorial provided a window onto how the problem of youth violence would be framed for the rest of the decade.

Despite the research from Washington, D.C. and elsewhere that some violence prevention programs targeting children and youth during peak hours for victimization and perpetration are successful, William Bennett, John DiIulio, and John Walters would, by 1996, write of urban super-predators: "for as long as their youthful energies hold out, they will do what comes naturally: murder, rape, rob, assault, burglarize, deal deadly drugs, and get high." This dire predictive model was also premised on the belief that because the US youth population was expected to grow by between fifteen and twenty percent over the next decade that the rate of violent crime would increase. And, as they noted, this was a problem "especially among young urban minority males."

Begging the question "Do they commit more crime?" cultural conservatives continue to use arrest rates to justify harsher criminal justice interventions for youth without any consideration of how the "front" and "back" doors of the system disproportionately impact youth of color at every stage of the process. Largely ignoring the discrimination, including class, gender, and racial biases in the criminal (adult and juvenile) system, they are blind to the lack of media attention to white juvenile delinquency, as well as the discretion that sometimes benefits white youth by diverting them from the juvenile justice system.

The point is that there is enormous racial disparity and discrimination in treatment at all stages of the juvenile justice system, including at the point of diversion, arrest, detention, disposition, and in decisions to revoke probation. In Washington, D.C., for example, the juvenile justice system is 100% minority (BRC 2000). A comprehensive study of the juvenile justice system found that not one white kid had been detained or committed in a juvenile case in an eighteen months period spanning 2000 and 2001. The same study found that white youth are disproportionately diverted at the "front door" from entering detention status, even when they are facing more serious, violent Part I crimes.

Again, the increasing popularity in the mid to late 1990s of tales of urban youth who come from "criminogenic environments" – to use Bennett, DiIulio, and Walters' characterization – paralleled declines in violent crime, declines in youth homicide, declines in the percentage of violent crimes among youth crime, and increasing intake of youth convicted of drug crimes with no prior history of violence. Declines in youth violence and crime also took place in Washington, D.C. and Boston after substantial investments in afterschool programs, youth entrepreneurship programs, neighborhood service delivery improvements, diversion programs for minor offenses, and implementation of community-based alternatives to incarceration. Contrary to popular mythology, they were not solely the product of harsher sentences for youth.

In addition to an underrepresentation of black youth victimization in urban environments, one of the most overlooked points in this discourse as well is that youth did not and do not constitute the majority of arrests for violence crime. In a recent study, the Youth Law Center documented the pervasiveness of this stereotype, even though youth made up a small percentage of overall violent crime arrests. Their review of national media found that seven out of ten news stories on violence involved youth, while youth arrests made up only fourteen percent (14%) of arrests for violent crime. In Washington, D.C., an analysis in 2001 found that youth under eighteen years of age are responsible for just under six percent (6%) of violent crime in the city. An associated study also found that minority youth were depicted as perpetrators in excess of their offending rates, and that they were under reported as victims on news.

At bottom, the super-predator thesis legitimized and continues to inform calls for disinvestments in community-based prevention and youth development programs. This has also occurred amidst other studies, which increasingly document a more "scientific" authority in the call to end ameliorative social policy intervention. As early as 1993, an editorial in the *Chicago Tribune* in 1992 revealed the potential policy impact from contemporary tales when it wrote the following after tentative findings linking serotonin – a brain chemical – to aggression were released: "Violent families breed violent children. Violent children become violent adults... But science is discovering another cause of destructive behavior, which is at once frightening and fraught with hope. It is the biological component. This is frightening because it implies that violent behavior cannot simply be "un-learned" by improving a child's circumstance or by teaching the benefits of gentle cooperation. Those things must be done, but they are unlikely to totally undo that which has become biologically embedded." The *Tribune* and other media outlets would continue to provide authority for cultural conservatives who want to stereotype the landscape from which they contend that youthful, violent predators arise.

Alternative Frameworks for Framing Public Intervention

Important voices countering deterministic policies and perceptions of urban youth and environments have come from many sources, including youth themselves. The public health community remains especially vocal, even as some of its leading advocates reject more rigid biological and scientific formulations only to re-inscribe a cultural determinism Fergerson 1999; Hoberman 1997).[4] A recent report from Surgeon General David Satcher, however, reveals a more promising discourse. Frustrated with dire policy characterizations, Surgeon General David Satcher commissioned a study of youth violence in the United States to establish more authoritative empirical contextualization. In the recently released report entitled *Youth Violence: A Report of the Surgeon General*, Dr. Satcher proclaims that "an important reason for making research findings widely available is to challenge false notions and misconceptions about youth violence... Examples of these myths include: African American and Hispanic youths are more likely to become involved in violence than other racial and ethnic groups... A new, violent breed of young super-predators threatens the United States... Getting tough with juvenile offenders by trying them in adult criminal courts reduces the likelihood that they will commit more crimes... Nothing works with respect to treating or preventing violent behavior" (US DHHS 2001).

Surgeon General Satcher's documentation of effective community-based violence prevention strategies, however, has not yet succeeded in turning the tide of public policy. This is best reflected in the use of the waiver to adult court, where youth are sentenced as adults and commonly incarcerated with adults in a correctional setting. Over the past two years, almost two dozen states have passed laws making it easier to try children and youth as young as seven years old in adult court (Butts 2002). This is in spite of research documenting that incarceration of youth with adults produces youth who, when released, have a higher recidivism rate and, ultimately, commit crimes of greater severity. The adult system has also not done a better job "rehabilitating" children and youth, who are subjected to violence within adult prisons (Bishop 2000).

Conclusion

Tales and rumors framing policy and media discourse about urban youth continue to obscure important risk factors and high quality research regarding factors such as the importance of stable economic opportunity, quality education and quality out of school time programming in strategies for the prevention of youth violence and crime, and the ability of community-based programs to prevent further experience with a juvenile or adult criminal justice system (D.C. Children's Trust Fund 2002; Mendel 2001). Sadly, community-based investments in youth development have not kept pace at the same rate as investments in the construction of institutionalized settings. The public also continues to resist replication of detention reform strategies garnered from several places, such as Tarrant County, Texas, Chicago, Illinois, and Missouri, where diversion and deinstitutionalization of youth, as well as placement in community-based settings, has occurred with low recidivism and lack of escalation of youth violence rates.[5] Without more attention to the ways in which characterizations of urban youths in narratives of youth violence and crime remove proven investments for youth from the policy table, tales of the state(s), in some cases, will continue to undermine effective public policy.

In spite of the data illustrating the importance of out of school time programming with adult supervision, community-based mental health and substance abuse counseling and treatment, and the importance of youth development and anti-bias training for police officers, many poor spatialized and racialized youth live in communities where such investments are still lacking in significant ways. Without more attention to the ways in which characterizations of urban youth in narratives of youth violence and crime remove proven investments for youth from the policy table, tales of the state(s), in some cases, will continue to undermine effective public policy.

As this article approaches publication, the country is engaged in another public drama involving a youth and shootings. Informally dubbed the "sniper case", officials in the Washington, D.C. area are deciding the fate of a seventeen-year-old black, immigrant suspect who faces charges stemming from a series of fatal shootings in a number of jurisdictions (Kovaleski and Sheridan 2003). Amidst reporting that he is a boy who comes from "no roots", the media acknowledge that he was a bright student who was a "boy of bright promise". However, few stories reveal how the decision to bring charges in Virginia trumped the normal process for deciding which jurisdiction would take precedence. Nor do the media stories and pundits sustain criticism for the denial of an attorney to this youth or interrogate the fact that a public decision was made and sanctioned to try the first case in Virginia based on the ability to bring the death penalty more quickly for this particular teenager (Glod 2002).

In this particular case, the jurisdictional battle and the urgency of the decision by the United States Attorney to overrule Maryland and other jurisdictions reflects a public enactment of the framing of race and dangerousness in a powerful lynching discourse associated with the black youth suspect.[6] Following the denial of a conference between the youth and his defense attorney and a judicial decision to televise a transfer hearing (to determine evidence for pursuit in adult crime court), a Virginia juvenile court judge ruled in January 2003 that there is enough circumstantial evidence to try the youth as an adult (Glod and Jackman 2003). At bottom, the unfolding of the "sniper"-drama and this decision represent the culmination of efforts to blur – and, ultimately, remove – whatever remaining distinctions exist between juvenile and adult crime court.

Endnotes

[1] Data on school-associated violence are not systematically collected by the federal government. The National School Safety Center at Pepperdine University has been the prime source for these data, which are maintained on their website (http://www.nssc1.org/).

[2] Correspondence, Vincent Schiraldi to Blue Ribbon Commission on *Youth Safety and Juvenile Justice Reform*. Executive Office of the Mayor, Washington, D.C., Sept. 25, 1999.

[3] William J. Bennett, *et al.*, *Body Count*. New York: Simon and Schuster, 1996. 27-28. Again, these ideas are encoded in several media and policy discourses, including discussions of welfare, health, housing, and drug policy, etc. In their conservative tract, the authors offer policy prescriptions for dealing with urban super-predators by framing their cultural environments as being devoid of positive, asset-based influences that would make public investment in youth development and economic opportunity productive.

[4] Hoberman, in particular, reflects this tendency. He writes of a "black sports fixation" in *Darwin's Athletes*. This serves as a proxy for the black urban neighborhood.

⁵ Some of the models discussed in Mendel (2001), BRC (2001), and Demuro (1999) also recognize that many children and youths do not need to be under any supervision in the juvenile justice system, and that some cities and jurisdictions have been engaged in over-detention and over-commitment.

⁶ Although the name of the youth is widely known and invoked, I have chosen to honor the standard, if increasingly eroding practice, of guarding the name of a juvenile charged with a crime. The dishonoring of the best practice standard and publicly displaying unique identifiers for a youth is integral to my notion that this episode is being enacted as a lynching discourse. Akin to historical contexts in which lynching was more widely practiced in the United States, the frequent parading of the youth victim before news media and held in shackles by white marshals recalls earlier contexts in which the lynching of black men and women was enjoyed as public spectacle. For an extended discussion of how the practice and spectacle of lynching has intersected with notions of black masculinity, criminality, and sexuality, please see Phillip Brian Harper, *Are We not Men? Masculine Anxiety and the Problem of African-American Identity.* New York; Oxford: Oxford UP, 1996. 143-150.

Works Cited

Anderson, M.A., J. Kaufman, and T.R. Simon, *et al.* "School-Associated Violent Deaths in the United States, 1994-1999." *Journal of the American Medical Association* 286 (2001): 2695-2702.

Becker, Elizabeth. "As Ex-Theorist On Young 'Superpredators', Bush Aide Has Regrets." *New York Times* 9 Feb. 2001, National ed.: A16.

Bennett, William J., Jr. DiJulio, J. John, and John P. Walters. *Body Count: Moral Poverty and How to Win America's War Against Crime and Drugs.* New York: Simon and Schuster, 1996.

Bishop, Donna. "Juvenile Offenders in the Adult Criminal System." *Crime and Justice* 27 (2000): 81-168.

Blue Ribbon Commission on Youth Safety and Juvenile Justice Reform (BRC). *Final Report of the Blue Ribbon Commission on Youth Safety and Juvenile Justice Reform.* Washington: Executive Office of the Mayor, Nov. 6, 2001.

"The Boston Strategy to Prevent Youth Violence." http://www.bostonstrategy.com/

Bragg, Rick. "Bloodshed in a Schoolyard: The Impact; Determined to Find Healing in a Good and Decent Place." *New York Times* 27 Mar. 1998: A1.

Butterfield, Fox. "Racial Disparities Seen As Pervasive in Juvenile Justice." *New York Times* 26 Apr. 2000: A1.

Butts, Jeffrey A. *Trying Youth as Adults – An Overview of the Issue.* Washington: Urban Institute, 2002.

Cole, David. *No Equal Justice: Race and Class in the American Criminal Justice System.* New York: New Press, 1999.

Connolly, Ceci, and Dan Balz. "On the Trail, Subdued Discussion of School Violence." *Washington Post* 21 Apr. 2000: A2.

Davis, Angela. "Incarceration and the Imbalance of Power." *Invisible Punishment: The Collateral Consequences of Mass Imprisonment.* Eds. Marc Mauer and Meda Chesney-Lind. New York: New Press, 2002.

Demuro, Paul. *Pathways to Juvenile Detention Reform: Consider the Alternatives-Planning and Implementing Detention Alternatives.* Vol. 4. Baltimore: Annie E. Casey Foundation, 1999.

D.C. Children's Trust Fund. *Every Kid Counts in the District of Columbia: 9th Annual Fact Book.* Washington: D.C. Kids Count Collaborative for Children and Families, 2002.

Dorfman, Lisa, and Vincent Schiraldi. *Off Balance: Youth, Race, and Crime in the News.* Washington: Building Blocks for Youth, 2001.

Fagan, Jeffrey, and Franklin E. Zimring, eds. *The Changing Borders of Juvenile Justice: Transfer of Adolescents to the Criminal Court.* Chicago: U of Chicago P, 2000.

Feldman, Lisa, Michael Males, and Vincent Schiraldi. *A Tale of Two Jurisdictions: Youth Crime and Detention Rates in Maryland and the District of Columbia.* Washington: Building Blocks for Youth, 2001.

Fergerson, Gerard. "Tales of Black Criminality: Racial Determinism and Fatal Narratives." *Tales of the State: Narrative in Contemporary U.S. Politics and Public Policy.* Eds. Sanford F. Schram and Philip T. Neisser. Lanham: Rowman and Littlefield, 1997. 125-138.

---. "Cell Blocks." *First of the Month*. New York: First of the Month Collective, Jan. 1999.

Finn, Peter, and Erik Schelzig. "Violence of School Massacre Mystifies Germany." *Washington Post* 28 Apr. 2002: A23.

Gilliam, Frank D. *Youth Crime and the Superpredator News Frame: The Impact of Television on Attitudes About Crime and Race*. Washington: National Funding Collaborative on Violence Prevention, 2001.

Glod, Maria. "Malvo Team to Review Some Police Interviews; Defense Calls Ruling In Sniper Case a Win." *Washington Post* 31 Dec. 2002: B1.

---, and Tom Jackman. "Malvo Can Be Tried as Adult: Ruling Makes Sniper Eligible for Death Sentence." *Washington Post* 16 Jan. 2003: A1.

Griffin, Patrick, Patricia Tobert, and Linda Szymanski. *Trying Juveniles as Adults in Criminal Court: An Analysis of State Transfer Provisions*. Washington: Office of Juvenile Justice and Delinquency Prevention, Dec. 1998.

Harper, Phillip B. *Are We Not Men? Masculine Anxiety and the Problem of African American Identity*. New York; Oxford: Oxford UP, 1996.

Hawkins, Darrell F. "Ethnicity, Race, and Crime: A Review of Selected Studies." *Ethnicity, Race and Crime: Perspectives Across Time and Place*. Ed. Darrell F. Hawkins. Albany: State U of New York P, 1995. 11-45.

Hoberman, John. *Darwin's Athletes: How Sport Has Damaged Black America and Preserved the Myth of Race*. Boston: Houghton Mifflin, 1997.

Kenworthy, Tom. "Up to 25 Die in Colorado School Shooting." *Washington Post* 21 Apr. 1999: A1.

Kovaleski, Serge, and Mary Beth Sheridan. "A Boy of Bright Promise and No Roots." *Washington Post* 12 Jan. 2003: C1.

Mendel, Richard. *Less Cost, More Safety: Guiding Lights for Reform in Juvenile Justice*. Washington: American Youth Policy Forum, 2001.

"The New Biology of Violence." *Chicago Tribune* 19 Dec. 1993, Section 3:2.

Puritz, Patricia, Alycia Capozello, and Wendy Shang, eds. *More Than Meets the Eye: Rethinking Assessment, Competency and Sentencing for a Harsher Era of Juvenile Justice*. Washington: American Bar Association Juvenile Justice Center, July 2000.

"Report Details Wide Disparities in Juvenile Justice System." *Washington Post* 26 Apr. 2000: A7.

Rimer, Sara. "Terror in Littleton: The School; Good Grades, Good Teams and Some Bad Feelings." *New York Times* 26 Apr. 2002: A1.

"Speaking Out: The Legacy of Columbine." *Washington Post* 20 Apr. 2000: C4.

Schram, Sanford S., and Philip T. Neisser, eds. *Tales of the State: Narratives in Contemporary U.S. Politics and Public Policy.* Lanham: Rowman and Littlefield, 1997.

Stone, Deborah. *Policy Paradox: The Art of Political Decision-Making.* New York: W.W. Norton, 1997.

United States Department of Health and Human Services (US DHHS), Office of the Surgeon General. *Report on Community Forums – Youth Violence and Public Health.* Washington: US DHHS, Dec. 14, 2001.

---. *Youth Violence: A Report of the Surgeon General.* Washington: Government Printing Office, 2001.

"Young Black Men." Editorial. *New York Times* 7 May 1992: A26.

The African American Male Leadership Academy: A Case Study in the African American Experience

Jacob U. Gordon

The turbulent voyage of the peoples of African descent has been well documented in American life and history (Franklin 1994; Hayes 2000, Du Bois 1903; Woodson 1933; Hughes 1962; Herskovits 1966; Blassingame 1972; Bell 1998; Gordon 2000; Hailey 1976; West 1993; de Tocqueville 1835; Myrdal 1944; Williams 1944; to name a few). The black experience in America is the history of the struggle to translate America's promise into reality: "We hold these truths to be self evident that all men are created equal; that they are endowed by their creator with certain unalienable rights; that among these are life, liberty, and the pursuit of happiness." These were the immortal words of the third president of the United States, Thomas Jefferson, the principal author of the American Declaration of Independence. These words were the foundations on which America as "one nation, indivisible with justice for all," was built. It should be noted here that the legacies of the Trans-Atlantic slave trade and slavery continue to be a major hindrance to the fulfillment of America's promise. Admittedly much progress has been made, but much remains to be done in securing civil human rights for all Americans. The research for freedom and equality by African Americans continues to be a major challenge to American democracy. The African American Male Leadership Academy is a step toward American promise.

The plight of African Americans has been a subject of research and search for solutions for more than a century. Foreign scholars like Alexis de Tocqueville and Gunnar Myrdal were concerned about the future of African Americans in America. George Williams' two volumes, *History of the Negro Race in America* (1888), provide a clear picture of the African American problem. The African American male circumstances have been particularly disturbing: Wilkinson and Taylor (1977), Gordon and Mayors (1994), Staples (1982), Gibbs (1988), and Austin (1996) have revealed alarming data and trends about the status of African Americans.

The publication, *Repairing the Breach* (Austin 1996), provides other alarming data on the status of African American men and boys. A national Task Force Report under the sponsorship of the W. K. Kellogg Foundation, among other things, concludes that

"African American males (and the larger African American community) have faced continuous forms of mistreatment and oppression. The denial of the opportunities, and other related forms of racial discrimination all reflected practices and policies deeply rooted in American thought and American traditions. And the consequences of these historical practices are still very much with us today."

Other sources of research data confirm the conclusion of the Task Force as they reveal the following statistical overview of the status of African American men and boys:

Population
- The total U.S. population is 248,709,872. The total African American population is 29,930,524 (12 percent). Of this number, 14,170,151 are males (US Census 1990).

Health
- Black male life expectancy in 1991 was 64.6. White male life expectancy in 1991 was 72.
- The black male death rate for HIV in 1991 was 52.9, while the male death rate for HIV in 1991 was 16.7.
- Black males are more likely to be born to unwed teenage mothers who themselves have limited education and even more limited life choices (Gibbs 1988).

Homicide
- Homicide rates in 1991 for African American males were 72.5 per 100,000, nearly eight times higher than for white males (FBI 1993).

Poverty
- The rate of poverty for all African Americans was 29.5 percent compared to 9.8 percent for whites (US Census 1992).
- Nearly half (42.7 percent) of black youth under 18 live in families below the poverty line (Curtis 1996).

Family Life
- Of the 7,055,063 black families, 3,045,283, or 43 percent were headed by black females. Of all black families, 26.3 percent lived in poverty, compared to 7.0 percent of white families (US Census 1992).

Incarceration
- Almost one in three (33 percent) black males between the ages of 20 and 29 is under the supervision of the criminal justice system — in prison, jail, on probation, or on parole. This compares with one in sixteen white males and one in ten Hispanic males (Maurer 1990).
- The number of African American males in prison and jail exceeded the number of African American males enrolled in higher education (Maurer 1990).
- Black men in the United States were imprisoned at a rate four times that of black men in South Africa: 3,109 per 100,000 compared to 720 per 100,000 (Morton and Snell 1992). Forty-four percent of all prisoners in the United States were black; black men made up 40 percent of the condemned on death row (Sentencing Project 1990).

Education
- More than 20 percent of black male adolescents in the 12-17 age group were unable to read at the fourth grade level (Brown 1979).

Stereotypes
- The black male has been more negatively portrayed in the media and in literature than any other group in American history (Drake and Cayton 1945; Gibbs 1988).

Jobs
- Unemployment among black youth was 34 percent – twice the rate of 17.4 percent among all teenagers (Gibbs 1988).

By most social indicators – mortality, health, crime, homicide, life expectancy, income, education, unemployment, and marital status – African American men have the smallest chance to achieve the American dream. In fact, of the four comparison groups (black males, black females, white males, white females), social indicators showed that black males experienced the highest rate of health and social problems, including heart disease, hypertension, diabetes, homicide, suicide, unemployment, delinquency and crime, school dropout, imprisonment, and unwed teenage parenthood (Gordon and Majors 1994). As Gibbs reported, black males have been miseducated by the education system, mishandled by the criminal system, mislabeled by the mental health system, and misread by the social welfare system. In fact, she argued that black males had become rejects of the American affluent society and misfits in their own communities.

"African Americans in public schools are isolated and receive inferior educations despite forty years of federal and state efforts to provide equal opportunities." That was the conclusion of a recent report by the Committee of Policy for Racial Justice, a study group convened by the Washington-based Joint Center for Political Studies. Among other things, the report revealed two main educational barriers: 1) lowered expectations for African Americans and other racial minority groups, and 2) false assumptions of academic and intellectual deficiencies. The report also concluded that African Americans and other minorities are disproportionately placed in "lower-ability, non-college-bound tracks." The situation (according to the report) is compounded by a shrinking number of African American teachers (7 percent), curriculums that fail to include African American and other minority contributions, and inequities in standardized testing.

By virtually every official index – mortality, crime, homicide, life expectancy, income, education, unemployment, and marital status – African Americans emerge as one of the most troubled segments of American society. While African Americans account for 12 percent of the US population, they account for 50 percent of the nation's prisoners. Nearly nine of ten black inmates are male and 54 percent are below age 29. According to former Health and Human Services Secretary Dr Louis W. Sullivan, "not since slavery has so much calamity and ongoing catastrophe been visited on black males."

A recent survey and review of literature on the current status of African American children and youth in gifted education programs reveals an underrepresentation of African Americans. While most educational programs are rightly concerned about dropouts, low achievers, and the disproportionate number of African American men in our prison system, few if any education programs are concerned about highly motivated honors and gifted African American youth. There is a tendency in the African American community to defend the underdog and neglect those who have the potential to pursue excellence in education. We often argue that the bright boys and girls will make it anyway. The data now suggests that the bright boys and men are making it in prison.

Figure 1

State of Missouri and Kansas City Population Distribution

	Race					
	One Race					
Geographic Area	Total Population	Hisp.	White	Black/AA	Asian	Others
Missouri	5,595,211	118,592	4,748,083	629,391	61,595	37,550
*Kansas City	441,545	30,604	267,931	137,879	8,182	14,158

*Source: Census Area Profile, Kansas City, Missouri.

Figure 1 (continued)

2000 Census Data

Urban Core Defined as Missouri River, Stateline, 75th Street, I-435 Hwy

(2) Population and Target Area

Ethnic Group	All Ages					Under 18 Years Old	18 Years Old or Over
White	160,805	49.80%	2,7665	34.50%	133,140		55.10%
Black	133,336	41.30%	43,684	53.90%	89,652		37.10%
Native American	1,530	0.50%	360	0.40%	1,170		0.50%
Asian	5,810	1.80%	1,279	1.60%	4,531		1.90%
Pacific Islander	351	0.10%	113	0.10%	238		0.10%
Other Races	1,519	3.90%	4,283	5.30%	8,236		3.40%
More than 1 race	8,455	2.60%	3,501	4.40%	4,864		2.00%
Total	311,806	100.00%	80,885	100.00%	341,831		100.00%
Hispanic (of any race)	25,544	7.9%	8,597	10.60%	16,947		7.00%
Minority (non-White or Hispanic)	172,622	53.50%	56,586	69.60%	118,036		48.00%

The Kansas City urban core is similar to other inner cities in many ways. It is surrounded by suburbs and rural communities. According to the *Metro Outlook* (2001), a publication measuring the problems of metropolitan Kansas City, a quality of life analysis by race indicated disparities between whites and non-whites. It reported a significant difference in perceived quality of life between white and non-whites. Only 74 percent of non-whites expressed satisfaction with their quality of life compared to 87 percent of whites.

Figure 2
Quality of Life by Race
White/Non-white Proportion by QOL Quintile

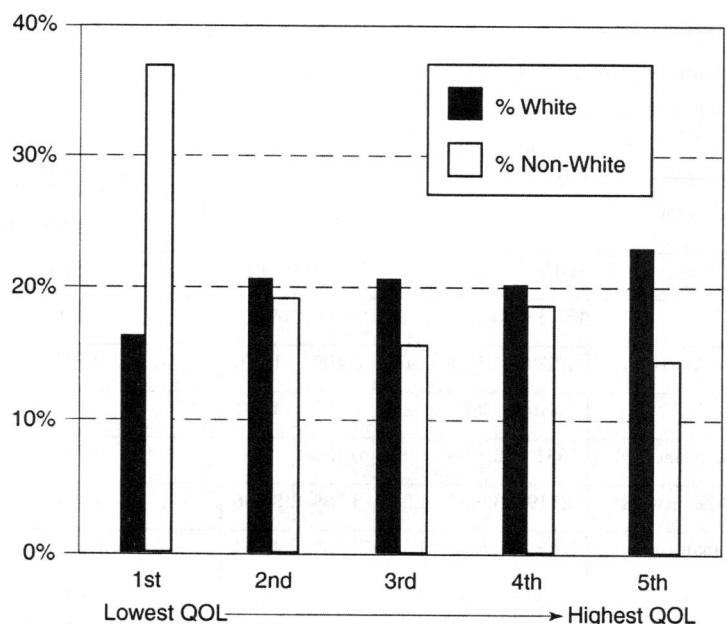

Source: Metro Outlook Public Survey

Related to quality of life is the disparity in poverty level. Figure 3 shows the extent of the disparity.

Figure 3

	Above Poverty		Below Poverty		Poverty Rate	
	White	Black	White	Black	White	Black
Total	1,161,892	138,170	84,233	53,865	7%	39%
Total living in census tracts with poverty ≥ 20%	50,251	71,345	15,095	42,591	—	—
Percentage living in concentrated poverty areas	4%	52%	18%	79%	—	—

Other indicators of risk factors in the target area are reflected in the Missouri Department of Elementary and Secondary Education (MODESE) annual report of school data, compared to the rest of the state of Missouri. Figure 4 shows a five-year trend in the dropout rate. Figure 5 shows a five-year trend graduate analysis. Both sets of data reflect poor academic performance. It is not surprising that the Kansas City, Missouri school district lost its state accreditation in 2000.

The demographics of the Kansas City urban core and related task factors are likely to encourage substance abuse. The target area is characterized by poverty, low quality of life, academic failure, and hopelessness.

Figure 4

Annual Dropout Rate, 1997-2001

As a Percent of Total Enrollment

	Kansas City 33				
Year	1996-97	1997-98	1998-99	1999-00	2000-01
Dropouts 9-12	808	717	688	816	498
Dropout Rate 9-12 (%)	10.3	9.0	8.8	10.8	7.0
	Missouri				
Year	1996-97	1997-98	1998-99	1999-00	2000-01
Dropouts 9-12	13,880	12,974	12,114	11,415	11,941
Dropout Rate 9-12 (%)	5.5	5.0	4.7	4.3	4.5

Source: Missouri Department of Elementary and Secondary Education.

Figure 5

Graduate Analysis, 1997-2001

Year	Kansas City 33					Missouri				
	1996-97	1997-98	1998-99	1999-00	2000-01	1996-97	1997-98	1998-99	1999-00	2000-01
Total Number of Previous Year Graduates	1,132	1,120	1,181	1,130	1,053	48,418	50,175	51,926	52,189	52,433
Percent of Graduates										
Entering a 2 yr or 4 yr College/ University	8.04	22.68	22.44	22.39	30.29	51.33	52.00	52.30	53.91	54.46
Entering a Post-Secondary (non-college) Inst.	0.88	1.61	1.95	1.95	3.32	3.77	3.98	3.93	4.01	3.61
Entering the Work Force	12.72	29.64	32.77	29.47	23.74	32.61	32.61	32.01	31.70	31.00
Entering the Military	0.80	1.61	1.95	1.95	3.04	4.33	4.03	4.23	3.52	4.01
Entering Some Other Field	4.51	44.46	25.06	30.09	47.01	6.21	5.41	5.32	5.44	5.27

Source: Missouri Department of Elementary and Secondary Education.

As submitted to Core Data by Missouri Public Schools. Data as of November 20, 2001.

Cause and Effect

The question of causation and/or why the African American Leadership is relevant to this paper provides a basis for cause and effect analysis. Let us address the why-question first.

As to the explanation for the conditions of African Americans, three schools of thought may be examined: the liberal structuralist, the conservative behaviorist, and the conspiracy theorist. The literature over this debate is relatively extensive. It may be summarized in the following chart.

The Plight of Black America:

A Theoretical Framework

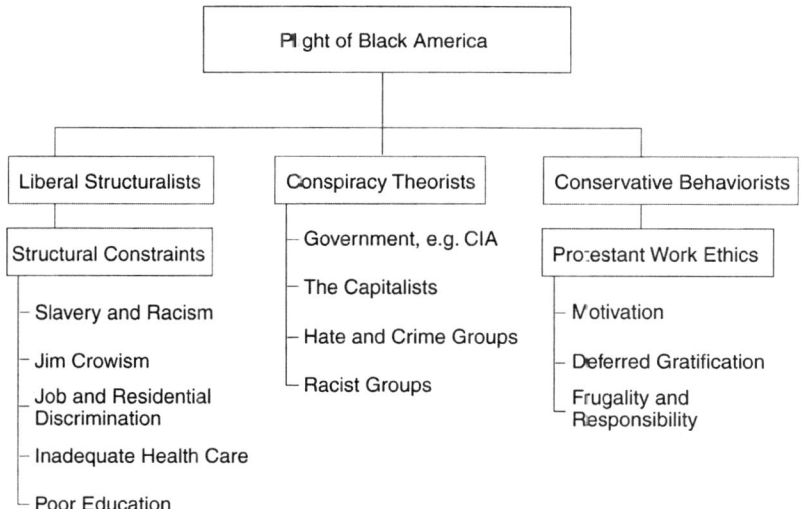

It is doubtful as to whether a single causation theory as summarized here can provide an adequate explanation for the current situation of African Americans. Neither the two extreme schemas nor the conspiracy theory can fully explain the situation. Noted, they have raised additional questions. For example, what constitutes a conspiracy against black Americans? Is racism a conspiracy against blacks? Is there a distinction between organized and unorganized conspiracies? A recent book by an American right-wing leader, Patrick Buchanan, *The Death of the West* (2002), argues against migration of people of color. Drawing on UN population projections, recent US Census figures and expert policy statements, Buchanan predicts the decay of Europe and America, and the decline of western civilization. He goes on to suggest that if not checked, people of color and the dying American and European populations will destroy western civilization. This appeal to Far Right conservative groups sounds familiar to note — the rise of the Ku Klux Klan and other hate groups in American history. Based on current available sources, it is safe to conclude that a thorough search for causation points to two directions: individuals and society. This may be translated to be individual African Americans and the American society, including institutions and systems.

A *New York Times* bestseller, *Losing the Race* (2001), by an African American scholar at Berkeley, John McWhorter acknowledges racism as an important factor responsible for the current status of African Americans. However, he warns that racism's ugliest legacy is the disease of defeatism that has infected black America, a kind of self-sabotage. McWhorter explores what he describes as three cultural viruses in the black community that are making blacks their own worst enemies in the struggle for success. These are the cult of victimology, separatism, and anti-intellectualism.

Program Content:
Purpose

The purpose of the African American Male Leadership Academy is to enhance the quality of life of African American men and boys and their families.

Goals and Objectives
- To provide African American children and youth with the academic and social skills to succeed in our society.
- To prepare African Americans for creative and effective leadership as role models in African American communities.
- To develop character in African American children and youth.
- To develop in African American men and boys a sense of belonging through active participation in family and community affairs.
- To help African American men and boys understand, appreciate, and promote the cultural heritage of the black community.

- To help African American youth pass from individual status to that of an integrated member of the society and community by adopting the concept of collectivism as opposed to individualism.

Core Curriculum

The core curriculum is based on seven competencies: 1) service to humanity, 2) comprehensive knowledge of American social history, 3) literacy, 4) entrepreneurship, 5) world view, 6) citizenship education, and 7) compassion. It incorporates integrated humanities and arts, math and the sciences, social studies, health and family education, and leadership training. It covers Africa as the cradle of civilization; African cultures, values, and rites of passage; achievements in the African past, including Egyptian civilization and the ancient kingdoms of Africa and contributions of peoples of African descent in World history. An annual black Leadership Symposium at the University of Kansas culminates the Academy's activities. Successful African Americans serve as role models and mentors to program participants.

- *Humanities and the Arts.* Each curriculum area integrates related disciplines like literature, philosophy, religion, communication skills, reading and writing skills, music, art, comparative systems of law, drama, and language in African and African American history and culture.
- *Math and* Science. History and the origins of mathematics and the sciences emphasize scientific methods of inquiry in physical and natural sciences. Issues essential to understanding *advanced* science will receive major attention. There will be a major emphasis on computer literacy through 1) basic electronics, microprocessors, and computer technology; 2) how to build and use personal computers; and 3) computer programming. A computer lab will be established for project participants.
- *Social Studies.* Geography, politics, leadership (biographies), psychology, sociology, anthropology, and government will include contemporary political issues with a focus on US history. An in-depth study will cover periods of conflict and change as well as ongoing social movements as they relate to justice, democracy, community, and individualism. Issues of governance and power will be central.

- *Health and* Family *Education.* Health and family related issues: sex education, issues of alcohol and other drug abuse, conflict resolution strategies, and related social and ethical concerns, will be included.

Leadership Training and Employment Preparation Services (EPS)
Today's leaders face the task of turning the work of the community back to the community. Leadership mobilizes groups to do work. This demands innovation in defining problems, generating solutions, and locating responsibility for defining and solving problems. Training includes the importance of shared leadership or rotating leadership, while reorganizing formal and informal leadership. Students will learn to solve problems and make decisions.

- *Summer Internship.* Eligible participants in the Academy will have opportunities for summer internships with participating community employers. The students will be carefully monitored during their tenures as interns. The purpose is to prepare them for the real world, the world of work.
- *Mentoring Program.* The program will give students skills to recruit potential mentors. Individuals will be encouraged to recruit mentors from family members, friends and acquaintances, service providers, employers, co-workers, peers, teachers, and community leaders.

Eligibility.
- African American male students, ninth grade (high school freshman)
- Must be "gifted" or have potential to succeed. "Giftedness" will include identification and referrals by teachers, school administrators, community leaders, peers, self-identification, religious leaders, parents, and community organizations such as the NAACP's ASTRO program or the Boys and Girls Clubs.
- Must demonstrate leadership potential.
- Must be in a post-secondary academic track/college-bound.
- Must be willing to provide community service by being a mentor to sixth, seventh, and 8th grade youth or volunteering in a black community literacy project.
- Must strive for parent/guardian involvement.

The Intervention Model

The model for intervention was based on three essential elements: leadership, linkages, and local data. Three sites were selected in Kansas and one urban site in Missouri. They were Topeka, Wichita, Kansas City, Kansas, and Kansas City, Missouri. The development of local leadership, linkages among local agencies, and the collection of local data were the three major elements for sustaining the program. This sustainability strategy produced three results. First, it provided opportunities for the community to "buy" into the vision of the program. Second, it enhanced community leadership, local ownership, and support for the program. Third, it addressed the issue of accountability through a systematic evaluation process. The model has been diagrammed as follows:

Program Model

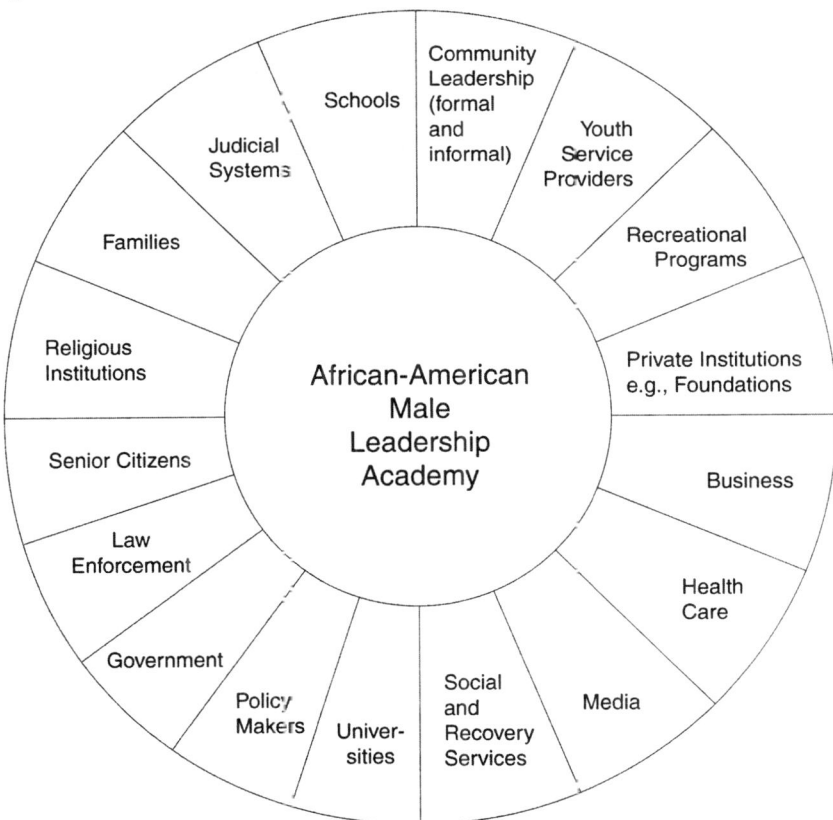

Leadership, Linkages, and Local Data

Program Evaluation

The basic logic model is used for evaluating the program. This evaluation process helps the program to address four related questions:

- What do we want to accomplish?
- What are we doing to accomplish it?
- What have we accomplished?
- What differences have we made?

The procedure involves four steps:

- Identifying goals, objectives, and desired outcomes (Step 1).
- Describing what activities have taken place to accomplish goals, objectives, and outcomes (Step 2).
- Describing what changes have taken place, whether the goals, objectives, and outcomes have been accomplished (Step 3).
- Documenting what difference the program has made (Step 4).

These four steps are diagrammed as follows:

Basic Logic Model

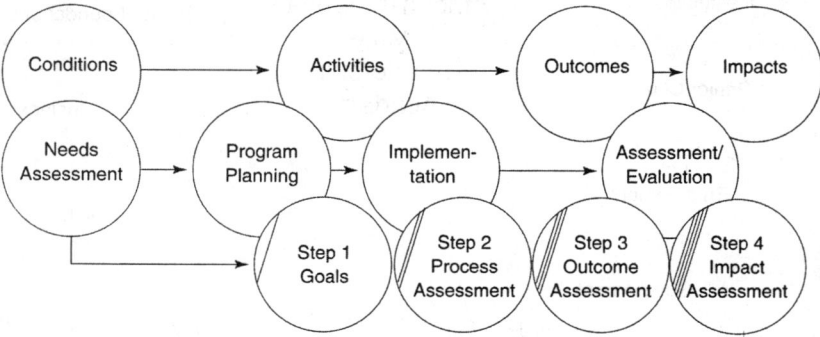

Impact Data

1. Have there been grade level increases?

    Yes, the 150 active participants in the programs since 1993 are all completing high school this year except one at the Wichita site.

The African American Leadership Academy

2. Has education increased?

    Yes, our records show that not only has formal education increased, but leadership skills and social skills. More than 80 percent of the participants have increased their school grades and ACT/SAT scores.

3. Are the participants staying out of trouble?

    Yes, in general. However, it is important to note that since the inception of the program two boys were caught in the juvenile justice system.

4. Has attendance increased?

    Yes. Both school attendance and program activities during the year ending in May 2002 is at 95 percent.

5. Has job development increased?

    Yes, more than 90 percent of the participants have part-time jobs and/or internships. The appointment of community resource coordinators has made this significant accomplishment possible.

6. Have participants been able to find jobs?

    About 95 percent of those seeking jobs were able to find jobs. Fifty percent or more have paid internships. The latter is our preference.

7. Other relevant data:

    - 99.3 percent high school completion rate for the Academy's first graduating class.
    - 95% will pursue post-secondary education, both in-state and out of state.
    - Twenty-six cadets currently serve as mentors to pre-school age African American boys.
    - Cadets Speakers Bureau in Wichita conducts workshops on leadership in six middle schools.

Outstanding Individual Achievements

Topeka Site

1. Sterling Barnes: Selected among 300 students nationally to study abroad, Germany.
2. Alfred Jackson: Topeka High, scored 4.0, Upward Bound high achievement.
3. Richard Edward: Highland Park School's special award for accomplishment in music.

Wichita Site

4. Vincent Edwards: Construction Company Scholarship $750
KU Academic Scholarship $4,000
Kemp Scholarship $300
Link Scholarship
African American Legislative Caucus Scholarship

5. Elliott Swinney: LMK Youth Leadership Award
Western Union Scholarship
KU Leadership Symposium
Letter in track (4 years)
Letter in football (2 years)

Kansas City, KS Site

6. David Brown: Sumner Academy
International Baccalaureate Candidate
Member of National Honor Society
Member Team Leaders of Hope
Spanish Honor Society
US Marine Corp Scholarship
Catholic Social Service Club Volunteer
Scholarship to Purdue University (Engineering)

7. Corey Harris: First Chair Saxophone in the Jazz band and Blues combo
Honor Roll
Member of Usher board, church

8. Damien Banks: Sumner Academy
Letter in Football
Chamber Singers
Member of Barbershop Quartet
Member of Drama Club
Parliamentarian: Jack and Jill of America
President of Youth Group at church
NAACP Youth Organization
Scholarship to Langston University (Computer Science)

9. Floyd Hawkins: Officer in Latin Club

The African American Leadership Academy

                    Letterman in basketball and track
                    Jack and Jill of America
                    AAU Citywide basketball team
                    Scholarship to Langston University (Business Management)

Kansas City, MO site

10. Bill Talbert: North East High
                    Member of Debate Club
                    NAACP Youth Organization
                    President of junior class
                    Scholarship to the University of Missouri at Kansas City (UMKC)
                    Letter in track and field
                    Honor Roll

11. Jermaine Reed: North East High
                    Board Member, MOVE UP, Inc (local community-based human service organization)
                    Broadcaster, local radio station
                    Honor Roll
                    Scholarship to the University of Missouri at Columbia
                    President, Urban Core Youth Group

12. Mohammed Katz: Southeast High
                    President of senior class
                    Honor Roll
                    Leadership Award by local Chamber of Commerce
                    Scholarship to Howard University in Washington, D.C.
                    Member, NAACP Youth Organization

Conclusion

Four major points are drawn from this study:

1. That it is possible to make a difference in the black American community through well conceived and effectively delivered programs such as the African American Male Leadership Academy.

2. That the African American Male Leadership Academy accomplishes its stated goals and objectives.

3. That the program is replicable, even across continental boundaries. And indeed the program is being replicated in other communities in the United States including the Chicago Housing Project; St Louis, Missouri; Washington, D.C.; and New York City areas.

4. At the time of writing the grants received from the W. K. Kellogg Foundation and the Village Foundation had ended. However, the institutionalization of the program on local levels was a fait-accompli. Thus the Academy continued to flourish with local support.

Works Cited

Austin, Robert, ed. *Repairing the Breach: Key Ways to Support Family Life, Reclaim Our Streets and Rebuild Civil Society in America's Communities*. Dillion, CO: Alpine Guild, 1996.

Bell, Derick. *And We Are Not Saved*. New York: Basic, 1987.

Blassingame, John. *The Slave Community: Plantation Life in the Ante-Bellum South*. New York: Oxford UP, 1972.

Buchanan, Patrick. *The Death of the West*. New York: St Martin's, 2002.

Du Bois, W. E. B. *The Souls of Black Folk*. New York: Bedford, 1903.

Franklin, John Hope. *From Slavery to Freedom*. New York: McGraw Hill, 1994.

Gibbs, J. T. *Young, Black, and Male in America: An Endangered Species*. Dover, MA: Auburn, 1988.

Gordon, Jacob, and Richard Majors. *The American Black Male: His Past, Present and Future*. Chicago: Nelson-Hall, 1994.

Hailey, Alex. *Roots*. Garden City, NY: Doubleday, 1976.

Herskovits, M. *The Negro World*. Bloomington: Indiana UP, 1966.

Hughes, Langston. *Fight for Freedom: The Story of the NAACP*. New York: Berkeley, 1962.

Kunjufu, J. *Countering Conspiracy to Destroy Black Boys*. Vol. 2. Chicago: African American Images, 1985.

McWhorter, John. *Losing the Race, Self-Sabotage in Black America*. New York: Perennial, 2001.

Myrdal, G. *American Dilemma: The Negro Problem and Modern Democracy*. New York: Harper and Row, 1944.

Staples, R. *Black Masculinity: The Black Male's Role in American Society*. San Francisco: Scholar Press, 1982.

Taylor, Roland, and Doris Wilkinson. *The Black Male in America*. Chicago: Nelson-Hall, 1977.

Tocqueville, Alexis de. *Democracy in America*. Trans. Henry Reece. Birmingham, AL: Legal Classics Library, 1935.

West, Cornell. *Race Matters*. New York: Vintage, 1993.

Williams, Eric. *Capitalism and Slavery*. Chapel Hill: U of North Carolina P, 1944.

Woodson, Carter G. *The Miseducation of the Negro*. Washington, D.C.: Associated Publishers, 1933.

Contradictory Policies and Their Implementation: Ethiopian Youth in Transition

Tamar Horowitz

The Ethiopian Jews, or Beta Israel (House of Israel), who came to Israel in the 1980s and 1990s were the first group of black Africans to arrive in Israel as full-fledged citizens under the Law of Return. It was not the first time that a minority with visibly darker skin had come to Israel; a group of Jews from Cochin, India, had arrived in the 1950s. But at that time they were part of a big wave of immigration from all over the world and were thus not as noticeable as the Ethiopian Jews in the 1980s and 1990s. Furthermore, they were a much smaller group.

There are many versions of the origins of the Ethiopian Jewish community. The different accounts have a bearing on the identity of the Ethiopian immigrants and on their acceptance by Israeli society. One version is based on folk traditions that say they are the descendants of Jews who went to Ethiopia during the reign of King Solomon or of Jews who were exiled after the destruction of the Second Temple. The second version is the historical-scholarly one. According to this version (Shabtay 1999, 32-33), Beta Israel emerged as a community in the fourteenth century. Before that time the dividing line between Judaism and Christianity in the African world was not very clear. Towards the end of the fourteenth century, Beta Israel set themselves apart from the rest of the African world by practicing different rituals and celebrating their own holidays, which were based on the Old Testament. In the other aspects of their lives, however, they were not much different from their neighbors (Pankhurst 1997). The consequence of their voluntary seclusion was hostility and harassment by their Christian neighbors (Kaplan and Solomon 1998). Though they defined themselves as Jews, they were isolated from the rest of the Jewish world. Their isolation from mainstream Judaism ended in the mid-nineteenth and early twentieth centuries, when European scholars introduced the Ethiopian Jewish communities to European Jewish organizations. As a result, a few attempts were made by groups of Ethiopian Jews to travel to Jerusalem on pilgrimages.

After the establishment of the State of Israel, some young Ethiopian Jews were sent by Jewish organizations to study in Israel, mainly in religious teacher-training institutions. The idea was that they would go back to teach Beta Israel children in

Ethiopia and strengthen the Jewishness of the community. In the 1960s and 1970s, various Jewish individuals and organizations tried to encourage the Ethiopian Jews to emigrate to Israel, but these were sporadic attempts that did not have the approval of the Israeli religious establishment (Weil 1995).

In 1977, Chief Rabbi Ovadia Yossef acknowledged the Jewishness of Beta Israel, claiming that they were descendants of the tribe of Dan and came under the category of Jews who belonged to the "banished tribes of Israel" (*nidhei Yisrael*). Because they did not know enough about the Jewish laws developed in the Middle Ages in Europe and in Moslem countries, they would have to undergo some sort of conversion, but nonetheless they were eligible to immigrate to Israel under the Law of Return. "No! You don't have to convert just because you don't know enough! The issue (although I don't know if he said it) was that, because they were unaware of Jewish laws pertaining to marriage and divorce, they might be *mamzerim*. To prevent this, they were to be considered non-Jews and would have to convert. These were not laws developed in the Middle Ages." In other words, the community was recognized as Jewish, but the Jewishness of the individuals needed correction (Kaplan and Solomon 1998). The Chief Rabbi's decision paved the way for the immigration of Jews from Ethiopia in the 1980s and 1990s.

There were two waves of immigration of Ethiopian Jews: Operation Moses, in 1984, in which eight thousand immigrants were brought to Israel, and Operation Solomon, in 1991, when fourteen thousand immigrants arrived. Between the end of Operation Solomon and 2000, another 46,600 Ethiopian Jews immigrated to Israel. The Ethiopian Jewish community in Israel numbers now 85,000 people.

Government Policies

From the beginning of the first wave of Jewish immigration from Ethiopia in 1984, the Israeli government was aware that policies and strategies that were applied to other groups of immigrants could not be applied to the Ethiopian Jews; policies had to be revised. This awareness among the absorption authorities did bring about some changes in the way the Ethiopian immigrants were perceived, but no coherent plan was developed for handling this new wave of immigrants.

In the first few years, a lot of energy was invested in gathering information about their life in Ethiopia. Some of the information was ethnographic: rituals, folktales, and material culture. Other information was more sociological and psychological:

information about individual behavior and about family and community structures and functions. The information gathered had two effects: it made a body of knowledge available to the agencies dealing with the immigrants, and it put a stigma on the community – that they were an exotic, primitive, illiterate community and that even their religious practices were far from those of mainstream Judaism. The gathering of information about the lives of the immigrants before they came to Israel was unprecedented; no other ethnic group in Israel had been the subject of such detailed research and questioning, and no other group had had so much information gathered about it.

A. Policies

Nine immigration policies had an impact on the integration of Ethiopian Jewish immigrants in Israel in general, and on the Ethiopian youth in particular.

The first policy was massive government intervention (Tsaban 1994). From the beginning there was an awareness that transforming a population group from an underdeveloped country so that they fit into a modern industrial society would require a large governmental investment over a long period of time. The government also realized that intervention meant more bureaucracy, less flexibility, and a lack of cultural sensitivity. Notwithstanding this policy, there were many voluntary associations and groups, from Israel and from the United States, that supported the new immigrants; but their support was not always compatible with government policies, and sometimes they duplicated services already provided by the government. In brief, resources were wasted.

The second policy was indirect absorption. This meant that the immigrants were referred temporarily to absorption centers, where they were supposed to learn Hebrew and how to manage in Israeli society. They learned about the labor market, and some underwent a retraining process; they learned about the social services, and those in need were directed to the appropriate service. Since many of them were carriers of the HIV virus, they were instructed about preventive measures.

Absorption centers had been an important mechanism in the integration of the Russian immigrants who came in the 1970s completely unprepared for life in a free-market society. They stayed in the absorption centers for less than a year and made good use of the information they received there to prepare for life in their new home. The case of the Ethiopians was very different. They stayed in the absorption centers for a long time because they could not find work; they were secluded from the rest of Israeli society; and they grew dependent on the bureaucratic system and its officials. They were labeled a problem group (Herzog 1998).

The third policy was settlement in Israeli urban centers. The memory of the Jews from Islamic countries who were directed to the periphery in the 1950s and 1960s and to this day remain the most disadvantaged sector of the Israeli Jewish population prompted the absorption authorities to choose this policy. The rationale behind resettling the Ethiopian immigrants in the urban centers was that their integration would be faster and better if they were sent to places with a strong infrastructure for employment, social services, and education. Another argument was that it was unfair to overburden the weak periphery with immigrants who needed massive help (Tsaban 1994). Many of the young people in the Ethiopian community argued that if the Ethiopians were sent to the urban centers, they would lose their self-confidence and be exploited by the stronger population. In the end, despite the generous mortgages given to the Ethiopians by the government, the policy was not a success because they were exploited by real estate agencies, settled in slum areas in the cities, and overpaid for their apartments. In a sense, those who went to the periphery were better off because they were concentrated in small towns and had a better community life and more interaction with the local population.

A related point is that the immigrants were not sent to agricultural localities. Many social scientists argued that the newcomers had bad memories of rural life in Ethiopia, where Jews were deprived of land to cultivate, and those who worked on the land were exploited by the owners. This was one of the reasons why the government did not offer them this option. Another argument was that Israeli agriculture was in a crisis, and there was no point in adding more people to a sector of the economy that was in a process of decline. On the other hand, some young people from the Ethiopian community argued that agriculture was a good solution for unskilled immigrants, at least for the adult generation.

The fourth policy was dispersal of the immigrants. The idea was to avoid creating black enclaves. No more than three Ethiopian families were supposed to be in one apartment building, no more than fifty families should be in a neighborhood, and Ethiopians should not constitute more than 4 percent of the population of a town.

Despite this policy, however, there are many towns in Israel where Ethiopians account for over 10 percent of the population; and there are enclaves in many towns that lead to antagonism and hostility between population groups. The principle of dispersal was also applied to schools. The Ministry of Education decided that pupils of Ethiopian origin should not account for more than 25 percent of any class, but in many schools there are more, mainly due to their residential pattern.

The fifth policy was empowerment of individuals and families; little attention was given to the community as such. The absorption authorities did not realize what the consequences of delegitimating their traditional leadership would be. It is worth mentioning in this context that the absorption authorities did not distinguish in their policies between different groups and communities of Ethiopians. They considered them one homogeneous group, and this contributed to the stereotyping of the community.

The sixth policy was to create a new leadership. This policy was the outcome of the Israeli religious establishment's decision not to recognize the Ethiopian spiritual leaders – the *kesoch* – as authorized rabbis for any purpose. In Ethiopia the *kesoch* performed weddings, funerals, and other rites and were influential community leaders. The consequence of the delegitimation of the *kesoch* by the religious establishment was a decline in the status of the old leadership, not only in religious matters but also in other social and community matters. Therefore, in the crucial period of integration the community-based pattern of leadership was shattered (Kaplan and Solomon 1998). To some extent the community was left without effective leadership.

A new young leadership started emerging in the mid-1990s. These new leaders were drawn from a group of young people who were students or graduates of higher education and those who had been active in demonstrations against the government's stance on conversions. It is noteworthy that at first the young leaders fought against the delegitimation of the *kesoch*; although many of them were nonreligious, they felt that the issue was not just a religious issue but a community one. The government's policy today is to encourage young leaders, and there are many mechanisms for the creation of such a young elite.

The "third sector" is also involved in building new leadership. The government gives financial support to the umbrella organization of the Ethiopian Jewish community (the UEJO). The new young leaders are involved in civic activities. Many of them are working on community development projects, educational improvement programs, and activities that promote understanding between Israelis and the new immigrants. However, they are divided among themselves, and it is sometimes very difficult for them to undertake a joint venture.

The seventh policy, based on a coalition agreement with the National Religious Party, was the enrollment of school-age children in State-Religious schools. In 1985 it was decided that the children would first go to State-Religious schools and would later decide for themselves whether they wanted to carry on in a State-Religious school or transfer to a nonreligious State school. The rationale was that this was a traditional and religious community, and the gap between them and society at large would be less conspicuous if they attended State-Religious schools. It is worth noting that the decision was made without consulting the community leaders or obtaining their consent. This decision was reversed after the Labor government came to power and the new Minister of Absorption encouraged the Ethiopians to enroll in secular schools. The main argument was that the quality of the secular schools was better, as they did not cream off the elite students and send them to *yeshivas*. Although most of the children stayed in the State-Religious schools, the number of children enrolled in nonreligious schools is increasing.

Another educational issue was that of boarding schools. It was recommended that adolescents between the ages of twelve and seventeen attend religious boarding schools. The argument was that, since their environment was very poor and their parents were busy finding their place in society and could not devote time to their children, it would be preferable for the children to be in boarding schools. There they would be sheltered and would have the opportunity to concentrate on learning academic subjects and social skills. It was also argued that young people in Ethiopia, like those in other African communities, were used to staying with their peers for long periods of time. As a result, until the early 1990s, some 80-95 percent of Ethiopians between the ages of twelve and eighteen attended religious boarding schools. This meant that the parents were not involved in the socialization of the younger generation, and the adolescents were deprived of family life.

Beginning in the mid-1990s, the trend changed. More and more adolescents attended local high schools, and only a third went to boarding schools. It is worth mentioning that during this time boarding schools changed their orientation towards the Ethiopian students. At first they concentrated on helping the students adjust to the educational setting; later the emphasis shifted to social skills and relationships with the Israeli students. Now the emphasis is on cognitive development. Years later, when many of the young people who had been educated in boarding schools were asked whether they would consider sending their children to boarding schools, nearly three quarters of them said no.

The eighth policy was affirmative action. Until the 1990s, affirmative action was not applied to any immigrant group or ethnic group; other mechanisms were used to enhance equality. In the case of the Ethiopians, the government came to the conclusion that only affirmative action would work (Horowitz 1996). This mechanism was employed in two areas: housing and higher education. Affirmative action was welcomed by the general public, who considered it an essential means for the advancement of the Ethiopians.

The ninth policy was preservation of the community's traditions. Because most of their tradition was oral, it was very important to interview the older people, but this was done at a slow pace. Kaplan and Solomon argue that such policies of cultural preservation proved to be mainly rhetoric and not realistic. It is also worth mentioning that, as of the mid-1990s, there were only two Ethiopian synagogues in Israel (Kaplan and Solomon 1998). Another aspect of preserving the culture was the celebration of the Sigd holiday, which commemorates the return from Exile mentioned in the books of Ezra and Nehemiah. This holiday received the legitimation of the state and was made a national holiday.

When examining the nine policies vis-à-vis the Ethiopian Jews, one can see that the Israeli government did not have a coherent model of integration for them. The government moved from an assimilationist orientation to a pluralistic orientation and back again. The dominant philosophy of the state since its establishment was to assimilate new immigrants as soon as possible into the dominant culture of Israeli society. This approach had been undergoing a process of change since the late 1970s, mainly because Israeli society had become more socially, economically and culturally heterogeneous, making it very difficult to define the dominant culture. As a result, Israel is far more tolerant today of group values, symbols, and rights.

In contrast with other ethnic groups, in the case of the Ethiopians there was strong pressure to go back to the assimilationist orientation, because the new immigrants came from a non-industrialized society and a rapid adjustment to modern industrial society was essential for their integration in the labor market and the learning of new concepts of citizenship. This meant demanding that the immigrants make some sacrifices and give up certain aspects of their identity by assimilating into the modern context. On the other hand, there was an awareness that Israeli society should respect the indigenous culture and religion of the Ethiopian Jews and be sensitive to their modes of behavior without being patronizing. The assimilationist model was easy to adopt because it is deeply entrenched in the philosophy of the Israeli absorption authorities. The other model, the pluralistic one, is more difficult to adopt, especially when the religious establishment demands integration on its own terms. The compromise was the adoption of an ethnic-additive model of integration, which involves incorporating some ethnic elements into the mainstream culture, but it is basically a modified version of the assimilationist model.

B. Youth Policies

The nine immigration policies had a direct impact on the integration of the younger generation. When the integration of the adults is problematic, there is a tendency to direct resources to the younger population. The notion of a "wilderness generation", which was widely cited in the 1950s, was brought up once again. The idea was that, like the Children of Israel who spent forty years in the wilderness after the Exodus from Egypt, the adult immigrants were not capable of adjusting to modern society.

The main elements of the youth policy in the 1990s were as follows: it is preferable that young people be integrated in schools in their own communities. It is more beneficial for young people not to be separated from their families, and it is better for the community because young people who are more familiar with Israeli society can strengthen the community. Students should be allowed to choose between religious and nonreligious schools. Talented students should be directed to high-quality academic schools. Students should be directed to academic tracks, and not mainly to vocational tracks. Mechanisms should be created to identify youth at risk. The diagnostic process that sent many of the young people to special education should be improved. Equal opportunities should be created for young Ethiopians in the army, and opportunities should be created for young Ethiopians so they can attend universities. An atmosphere of acceptance should be instilled among young Israelis.

The youth policies of the mid-1990s were more focused and more coherent than before and some of them derived from accumulated experience. As there are no comprehensive evaluations of the outcome of these policies, this paper will concentrate on findings from the last four years. The surveys and the research represent the situation at one point in time and do not reflect a process.

C. Surveys and Research Findings

Schools

In 1997 a study was conducted on a representative sample of 840 young Ethiopians between the ages of twelve and eighteen (Lifshitz, Noam, and Habib 1998). The findings showed that 18 percent were from single-parent families, and about a quarter were living in households with six children or more under the age of eighteen. Half had relatively old fathers – 55 years of age or more (Lifshitz, Noam, and Habib 1998, 9). Only 39 percent of the fathers had some form of education, 20 percent had one to eight years of schooling, and 6 percent had thirteen years of schooling. The implication was that they were not integrated in the labor market, and in fact, about two-thirds of the fathers were not working. Their knowledge of Hebrew was basic, which meant that the parents lacked the ability to communicate with their children's teachers (Lifshitz, Noam, and Habib 1998, 12).

As for school enrollment, it was found that State-Religious schools were still the main choice. Whereas in the 1980s 95 percent of the Ethiopian children attended State-Religious schools, 74 percent still attended religious schools in 2000, despite the policy encouraging them to attend nonreligious schools because of their higher academic standards (Svirski and Svirski 2002). As for their dispersal, the policy was that Ethiopian students should not account for more than 25 percent of a school's enrollment, but in reality things were different. It was found that 22 percent of the students were in classes in which more than 50 percent were Ethiopian; 33 percent were in classes that were 24-50 percent Ethiopian; 25 percent were in classes with 1-25 percent Ethiopians; and 5 percent were in classes in which all the children were Ethiopian (Lifshitz, Noam, and Habib 1998, 22).

By the late 1990s, boarding schools were no longer the preferred option. Only 36 percent of the age cohort attended them at the time, and most of these were youngsters from problematic environments whose families could not cope with life in Israel.

Significantly, when young Ethiopians were asked if they would send their children to boarding schools, about 70 percent reacted negatively (Svirski and Svirski 2002).

Tracking in the educational system had an effect on future prospects of integration. Some 55 percent of the students were directed to vocational tracks, 28 percent with the option of taking the matriculation exams. For the other 27 percent it was a dead end with no option of obtaining a matriculation certificate (Svirski and Svirski 2002).

The dropout rate among young Ethiopians (aged 14-17) was higher than among the general Israeli population. A survey conducted in 1997 (Lifshitz, Noam, and Habib 1998) shows that 6 percent of Ethiopians, compared with 2 percent of Israelis, drop out of school. The latent dropout rate was 5 percent. The dropout rate according to another survey (Svirski and Svirski 2002, 24-36) was 16.5 percent among those who immigrated between 1996 and 1999.

A matriculation certificate is a gateway to Israeli society in general and to higher education in particular. Some 33 percent of the Ethiopians who attended schools with an academic track that made them eligible for the matriculation examinations did receive a matriculation certificate in 2000, compared with 58 percent of Russian immigrants and 55 percent of Israelis. In 1997 only 20 percent of those enrolled in an academic/matriculation track passed the exams, and only 28 percent passed in 1998 (Saar 2001). The Lifshitz, Noam, and Habib study also gives an indication of the quality of life of the Ethiopian students at school. As for the social integration of the young Ethiopians, a majority of the students reported that their classmates were willing to help them and to accept them as they are. Most of them expressed satisfaction with the way they were treated. However, about 39 percent said that they were bullied by Israeli students. As for associating with Israeli students during school hours, three quarters of the Ethiopian students said they associated with both Israeli and Ethiopian students; about a third said that they do not have Israeli friends.

An important aspect of life for young people is their relationship with their parents. Parents of Ethiopian youngsters no longer play a significant role in their lives. However, young Ethiopians help their parents by looking after their brothers and sisters, doing the shopping and helping to clean the house. Although many mothers attend school meetings, they feel that they cannot communicate with the teachers. Many students feel that they have less respect for their parents than they used to have. There are more conflicts with parents and the atmosphere at home has become tenser (Lifshitz, Noam, and Habib 1998). Some young Ethiopians develop feelings of bitterness towards their parents because they were separated from them when they were sent to boarding schools.

Higher Education

As the number of young Ethiopians who receive matriculation certificates grows, so does the number attending institutions of higher education. In 1992 the absorption authorities decided to give Ethiopian students grants for five to six years that include tuition fees and living expenses. The route to higher education is not direct; most of the students go through pre-academic courses which help them to improve their grades, mainly in English and mathematics, and to adjust to life at university and college. In 2000, a total of 950 students were enrolled in pre-academic courses – 132 in universities and the rest in colleges.

In 1994 there were 153 Ethiopian students in the seven Israeli universities. Most were undergraduates; 17 of them were Ph.D. students. A total of 123 were studying humanities and social sciences, and nine were in paramedical fields. Very few studied engineering or natural sciences. In 1999, 553 were enrolled in the seven universities, including 478 undergraduates, 39 Ph.D. students, and 34 diploma students. A total of 407 were studying humanities and social sciences, thirty-nine were studying natural sciences, twenty were studying engineering, and fifty were in paramedical fields. The pattern of choosing a discipline did not change much between 1996 and 1999 (Svirski and Svirski 2002).

As for other forms of higher education, 59 students attended colleges between 1996 and 1999, mainly technological colleges. The growing number of students in academic institutions created a leadership reservoir. Many of the professionals working with the community are graduates or students of institutions of higher education. They work in schools and community centers and do voluntary work in the community. They are responsible for introducing new educational programs, and they have created a lobby calling for improvements in the educational system.

The Israeli Army

Service in the Israeli army is one of the symbols of belonging. The government policy was to encourage young Ethiopians to serve in the army, and in fact, 95 percent of young Ethiopians do so. 30 percent of them serve in combat units, which is a higher rate than among the general Israeli population, and they do this of their own volition. Some 25 percent serve in professional capacities and the rest as rank-and-file soldiers. In 1996 there were already 68 Ethiopian officers in the army. Despite their high motivation to serve, many suffer from loneliness and financial problems, and 25 percent do not complete their army service. There are many programs designed to help them to function better in the army. Many women serve in the army even though they can be released on religious grounds. In 1996, 150 women served in the army.

Malka Shabtay found that military service helps young Ethiopians to develop an Israeli identity. Nonetheless, this does not weaken their Ethiopian identity. As Shabtay put it:

> The experiences the soldiers went through in their lives, in addition to the evaluation and reevaluation they performed during the process of structuring their identity, could have caused an identity crisis. That, at least, was the assumption of those who met members of the community around the time of Operation Moses. But most of the soldiers did not go through such a crisis. There were identity conflicts, mainly between parents and children; there was a situation of identity confusion, a "diffusion of identity," but not a crisis. The reason was the soldiers' high self-esteem, based on their identification with the culture and heritage of the community and with the struggle to survive until their dream to go to Jerusalem was fulfilled. This allowed a high degree of cultural continuity in addition to the acquisition of new values, so there was no vacuum that could cause self-hatred, disintegration, or crisis. (Shabtay 1999, 205)

Labor Market

Svirski and Svirski examined the 15-24 age group in the labor market in 1999. The findings show that 13 percent of males aged 15-17 and 9 percent of females in the same age group participated in the labor force. These high rates reflect the high dropout rate among young Ethiopians. Of those in the labor force, 74 percent of the males and 44 percent of the females are employed. In the 18-20 age group, 10 percent of the males are in the labor force, and 16 percent of them are employed. This is because most of the males are in the military, and the 16 percent are those who neither study nor serve in the army. As for females, 31 percent are in the labor force, and of those, 69 percent are employed. This shows that the girls are less inclined to serve in the army, but they tend to enter the labor market.

Identity

In her study on Ethiopian youth, Tamar Dothan showed that there are three types of integration:

- *The integrative type*: young people who have integrated and are acquiring a new repertoire without disposing of the old one. In effect they are saying: I am not exactly Israeli or Ethiopian. My manners are Ethiopian and my language is Hebrew.
- *The marginal type*: the type that says: I don't find meaning in either of the two cultures.
- *The assimilative type*: the type that says: I feel Israeli, I smoke like an Israeli on the Sabbath, I watch TV on the Sabbath, but I go to Ethiopian weddings.

Malka Shabtay, in her illuminating studies on Ethiopian young people in various settings, argues that in the last few years we can trace fractures in their Israeli identity, following painful experiences they have gone through. The experiences mentioned by various scholars are the religious establishment's demand that they convert; the non-recognition of their traditional leaders; the scandal that erupted when it was discovered that blood donated by Ethiopian immigrants was being destroyed for fear of being HIV-contaminated; and the feeling of isolation in absorption centers and boarding schools. In other words, their identity formation became problematic because they felt that they were not welcome in their Promised Land.

In her study *Between Reggae and Pop*, Malka Shabtay found that 33 out of sixty young Ethiopians considered themselves first and foremost Jewish, twelve defined themselves as black, ten as Ethiopian and only five as Israelis. Shabtay was one of the first researchers to try to understand in depth the meaning of belonging to a black minority in a white society, an experience that was new to the Ethiopians. It is worth mentioning that the government always hesitated to deal with the skin issue on a national level, though there were many attempts to address it on the school level. Kaplan and Solomon argued that there is no institutionalized racism, but there is unofficial racial prejudice. Many young Ethiopians complain of color discrimination in job interviews or when they go to a discotheque. This feeling of discrimination has caused many of them to look for a black identity. Shabtay documents that young Ethiopians are looking for a new space and a new identity. They feel that their identity is linked with the black population and that they can demonstrate their identity through black music. The young people, she maintains, cross the boundary to an alternative space with new boundaries. The interaction with these musical styles creates mechanisms of setting boundaries between them and the others, between them and the establishment, between them and Israeli society at large. Through the music they create the persona of the "other". Identification with black music is much more than preferring one style of music to another; it is about survival and about finding shelter at a time when the family is not a safe port, and Israel, for them, is not the Promised Land.

Nonetheless, Jewish identity remains strong, although it is not sufficient to create identification with Israeli society (Shabtay 2001). It is very difficult to estimate how many young people cross over to the other space, but there is no doubt that this option exists in the minds of a majority of young Ethiopians.

Conclusions

The integration of the Ethiopian immigrants is a story full of contradictions:
- The general philosophy informing immigration in Israel in the 1990s was to encourage immigrants to preserve their culture and identity while gradually acquiring elements of the new culture. The desired society would be a pluralistic one in which each ethnic group had its place but also shared the common culture. In reality, the new immigrants were under constant pressure to integrate according to the assimilationist model. The rationale was rooted in the philosophy of modernization. It is difficult for a group from an underdeveloped county to modernize without losing at least some elements of their identity.
- The authorities who dealt with immigrants respected the fact that they were a religious community but delegitimated their religious leaders.
- There was strong emphasis on the family, but children were taken away from the family and sent to boarding schools.
- A public promise was made to preserve their oral culture, but no serious attempt was made to keep the promise.
- There was a policy of not creating large concentrations of Ethiopian pupils in local schools, but in practice many of them ended up attending homogeneous Ethiopian schools.
- Affirmative action was employed, but the road to higher education was closed to many Ethiopians because they did not have a matriculation certificate, since they had been directed to vocational tracks.
- The government policies were free of racism, but some sectors in Israeli society manifested racism, while others showed prejudice.

- The policy was to refrain from patronizing, but for the immigrants the absorption centers were a symbol of dependency and patronization.

These contradictions in the orientations of the different policies and attitudes explain why the identity construction of young Ethiopians was so complicated. We can trace four different reactions to this situation:

- The first is that of the young, new leaders who had served in the army and attended institutions of higher education. They developed a sense of service to their community. Their identity is both Ethiopian and Israeli, although there is evidence of a growing tendency to strengthen their Ethiopian identity.
- The second is a race-based reaction. These young people feel that their main identity is black and that they want to create a black community in Israel. They find a common language with African laborers who work in Israel and with the black Hebrews.
- The third reaction is that of those who stick to their religious beliefs and have moved into the national-religious milieu of Israeli society.
- The fourth reaction is a confused identity. Those belonging to this category feel marginal in Israeli society, neither Ethiopian nor Israeli. They are in the lowest class of Israeli society.

It is hard to tell how many people are in each category, but in the short run we can say that many Ethiopians have a confused identity today.

Works Cited

Dothan, T. "Jewish Children from Ethiopia in Israel: Some Observation on Their Adaptation Pattern." *Israel Social Science Research* 3.1 (1985): 97-103.

Herzog, E. *Bureaucracy and the Ethiopian Immigrants: A Dependency Relationship in Absorption Centers*. Tel Aviv: Cherikover, 1998 (Hebrew).

Horowitz, T. "Value Oriented Parameters in Migration Policies in the 90s." *International Migration* 34.4 (1996): 513-538.

Kaplan, S. *The Beta Israel in Ethiopia*. New York: New York UP, 1992.

Kaplan, S., H. Solomon, and J. P. R. Process. *Ethiopian Immigrants in Israel, Experience and Research*. London: Institute of Jewish Policy, 1998.

Lifshitz, C., G. Noam, and J. Habib. *The Absorption of Ethiopian Immigrant Youth in Multi-Dimensional Perspective.* Jerusalem: JDC-Brookdale, 1998 (Hebrew).

Pankhurst, R. "Beta Israel in Their Ethiopian Setting." *Israel Social Science Research* 10.2 (1995): 1-12.

Saar, R. "Matriculation Achievements of Ethiopian Students." *Ha"aretz* 7a (15 May 2001) (Hebrew).

Shabtay, M. *Best Brother.* Ramat Hasharon: Cherikover, 1999 (Hebrew).

---. *Between Reggae and Rap.* Ramat Hasharon: Cherikover, 2001 (Hebrew).

Svirski, S., and B. Svirski. *The Ethiopian Israelis: Housing, Employment, Education.* Tel Aviv: Adva Center, 2002 (Hebrew).

Tsaban, Y. "Opening Remarks at the Conference Immigration, Language Acquisition and Patterns of Social Integration." The Hebrew University, 1996.

Weil, S. "Collective Designations and Collective Identity among Ethiopian Jews." *Israel Social Science Research* 10.2 (1995): 25-41.

Constructive and Constraining Masculinities: Masculinities and Racialization in Young Londoners

Ann Phoenix

The British Context as Mainstreaming Multiethnicity

The fiftieth anniversary of the arrival in Britain, in 1948, of the troopship "Empire Windrush" inspired both celebrations of, and reflections on, the meanings and experiences of Caribbean migration to Britain. The very attention given to the "Windrush" in the British media underlined a crucial change in British society over the last fifty years: from the assumption of mono-ethnicity to being undeniably and inextricably "multiracial" and "multiethnic". Those who were, in the 1960s (and even in the 1970s), constructed as "dark strangers" are now represented throughout British society and make crucial contributions both economically and culturally. It is the beneficial nature of these contributions that was a major impetus for the coining of the term "Cool Britannia" as a new and more useful way to characterize British national identity while giving recognition to its multiethnicity (Leonard 1997). The new British Race Relations (Amendment) Act (2000), implemented in 2002, puts the onus on public institutions to show that they are not engaging in racialized discrimination. This suggests that alongside changes in media and cultural representations, there have been welcome changes in what the state (led by a Labour government) considers acceptable in a multiethnic society, there have been new approaches to (although less marked) research representations and, in the last decade, there have also been challenges to research constructions of British African Caribbean people as "newcomers" and "outsiders" whose difference from the white majority is inevitably problematic. While such constructions are still common, there are an increasing number of research projects that treat inclusion of people from a variety of ethnic groups as "normal".

Yet, while the fiftieth anniversary of the "Windrush" is appropriately cause for celebration and recognition of the dynamism of British society and peoples, it also allows an engagement with the contradictions in this optimistic and romantic story. For the children, grandchildren (and great-grandchildren) of the "Windrush" generation have not been engaged in straightforward progress from exclusion and being the objects of racism to inclusion and multiculturalism and celebration. Instead, their experiences are, and have been, riven with contradictions of what Phil Cohen (1988) has termed "multicultures" and "multiracisms", characterized by racist attacks and informal segregation as well as by increases in "mixed parentage" and syncretic style.

This paper identifies some of these contradictions as they relate to young people. In particular, it focuses on the racialized complexity and contradictions produced in the educational context and on the contradictions faced and produced for young black men as they negotiate masculinities at school.

Mapping Present Educational Inequalities

In Britain, national school educational statistics are being recorded by "race" and ethnicity only from 2002. However, a survey of 25 British local education authorities (LEAs) conducted by the Office for Standards in Education (Ofsted 1999) found that the performance of all minoritized groups is improving. However, Bangladeshi, Pakistani, black Caribbean and Gypsy Traveller children attain poorly at GCSE. Gypsy Traveller children's performance is the worst, and the performance of black Caribbean pupils starts well in primary schools, but shows a marked decline in secondary schools. In general, Ofsted found that girls from minoritized groups attain more highly than boys do.

Gillborn and Mirza (2000) found enormous local variation in attainment levels by ethnicity. Using data from 118 Local Education Authorities, they found that each of the minoritized groups they studied was the highest attaining in at least one LEA. Thus, black students were more likely to attain five GCSEs than white students in 11% of the LEAs; Indian students were more likely to do this in 83% of the authorities, as were Pakistani students in 43% and Bangladeshi students in 26% of the LEAs. Looking at trends in attainment levels over a ten-year period (1988-1997), they found that all ethnic groups had improved their performance at GCSE. However, African Caribbean, Bangladeshi and Pakistani students had periods where their attainment levels worsened as well as periods when it improved. Students of Indian origin have made the biggest improvements and now tend to do better than their white peers. Bangladeshi students have improved their attainment, but the gap between Bangladeshi and white pupils has not really changed. By way of contrast, the improvement of African Caribbean and Pakistani students did not allow them to keep pace with their white peers, and the gap between them and white students has increased. As in the Ofsted report, Gillborn and

Mirza found that inequalities in attainment worsen for African Caribbean students as they go through secondary school.

Although gender and education has recently become an issue of enormous popular concern to some journalists and commentators as boys' school attainment in relation to girls has worsened, Gillborn and Mirza argue that:

> ...The analysis reveals new inequalities: showing that black pupils from relatively advantaged backgrounds are little better placed, as a group, than white peers from manual backgrounds... In contrast to the disproportionate media attention, our data shows gender to be a less problematic issue than the significant disadvantage of "race", and the even greater inequality of class... it is important not to fall into the trap of simply arguing between various inequalities. All pupils have a gender, class and ethnic identity – the factors do not operate in isolation... In 1997 the gap between boys and girls attaining five or more higher grade passes was nine percentage points. The difference between managerial/professional and unskilled manual was 49 percentage points... The data highlight a particular disadvantage experienced by Pakistani/Bangladeshi and African-Caribbean pupils. Here the girls attain rather higher than their male peers but the gender gap within their groups is insufficient to close the pronounced inequality of attainment associated with their ethnic group as a whole (Gillborn and Mirza, 21, 23 & 24; authors' emphasis).

While most work has been carried out on racialized educational inequalities in school, there are also inequalities in higher education. The Census records highest educational qualifications and the 1991 Census was the first to record ethnicity in Britain. From analyses of these, Mortimore, Owen and Phoenix (1997) found that black-African and Chinese people were consistently among the best qualified and that black-Caribbean, Pakistani and Bangladeshi groups were consistently among the worst qualified. People born in Britain were as a rule less well qualified than those born outside Britain. In general, men were better qualified than women, with the exception of black-Caribbean women who were better qualified than were their male counterparts. John Richardson (2002) analyzed a database of all students enrolled at institutions of higher education in the United Kingdom in 1995-96, provided by the Higher Education Statistics Agency. He found that white students were much more likely than others to get "better" degrees.

Such findings indicate that "race", gender, social class and attainment are complicated, dynamic processes. Furthermore, they show that both ethnicity and "race" are simultaneously important since different ethnic groups from within the same racialized group fare differently. It follows that explanations for these results also have to be multi-faceted and nuanced. However, there is evidence that some teachers view children from minoritized ethnic groups differently from those from majoritized ethnic groups. Various studies indicate the prevalence of racism in schools (see the review by

Gillborn and Gipps, 1996). Some teachers have been found to treat black and Asian students in stereotypic or hostile ways and/or to assume that they have behavior problems (Connolly 1998; Griffin 1985; Lees 1986; Mac an Ghaill 1988; Ogilvy *et al.* 1990,1992; Sewell 1997; Sonuga-Barke *et al.* 1993; Wright 1992).

Support for the idea that ethnicity and social constructions of behavioral problems are interrelated is provided by an OFSTED (1996) report on exclusions from secondary schools. The evidence reviewed in the report indicates that white pupils who are excluded from school are more likely to have experienced trauma and to be below average achievement. They are generally excluded for being verbally abusive to their teachers. The picture was different for black pupils who were excluded; they were more likely to have above average achievement and to have been excluded for challenging their teachers' judgments.

It is not being suggested that children from minoritized ethnic groups never present problem behavior. Clearly some do, and over the course of school careers, some – particularly black boys – can become challenging to teachers in response to what they perceive as racism from teachers (Mac an Ghaill1988; Sewell 1997). From her study including over 900 children in four comprehensive schools in Oxfordshire, Hurrell (1995) argues that pupils' behavior is likely to have an important impact on how teachers treat them. Based on her findings, she suggests that ethnicity and social class play only a small part in teachers' reactions to students – although girls tended to be treated more leniently than boys. Yet, this raises the question of what may be causing different behavior. For example, Osler *et al.* (2002) found that sometimes black girls were excluded for physically retaliating against verbal racist bullying. While physical retaliation is not to be condoned, the reasons for its occurrence need attention in any consideration of racialization and education. Whether or not behavior does differ between ethnic groups, Gillborn (1990) found that teachers' expectations that children of African Caribbean origin automatically constituted disciplinary problems led to the possibility of escalating conflicts and poor relations. Frosh, Phoenix and Pattman (2002) found that many 11-14 year old boys considered that teachers treated boys and girls, black and white children unfairly different. Both these studies indicate that teachers and children are agents whose racialized and gendered constructions both arises from, and has an impact on what happens in classrooms.

Of course not all teachers construct parents and children from minoritized groups as problematic. Gillborn (1995) studied three secondary schools in different parts of Britain. In two of these schools, at least half of the pupils were from South Asian backgrounds, and the third, while predominantly white, drew about 15 per cent of their students from minoritized ethnic groups. These schools were committed to antiracist policies, and various members of staff had put a lot of work into developing antiracist strategies. In doing so, they had managed to gain support from white parents. Nevertheless, Gillborn suggests that: "Of particular concern is the way that a small minority of teachers express generalized views that depict African Caribbean students (as a group) as a greater threat to their authority." (183)

Nehaul (1996) conducted a study of 25 children of Caribbean origin and five of their teachers in primary schools in the British Midlands renowned for a commitment to equal opportunities. Only in three cases did teachers express concerns about the support for children provided by parents, and they did not express generalized negative perceptions of children from minoritized ethnic groups. Despite this, teachers mentioned poor behavior as a cause for concern in relation to 17 of the 25 pupils and good behavior for only two. Since there is evidence that teachers can view the same behavior differently when done by white and Asian children (Sonuga-Barke *et al.*), the question of differences in behavior, its causes and perception continues to require complex treatment.

Masculinities: Racializing Contradictory Positioning

Debates about differences in boys' and girls' educational performance often imply that improving educational performance simply requires an act of will on the part of boys if they are to keep up with girls. However, a focus on the everyday practices of young men demonstrates that the psychosocial processes in which they are located are complex and contradictory. This section draws on a study of 11-14 year old boys, interviewed on their own (78) and in groups (over 200), about masculinities to demonstrate how boys, as agents, negotiated these contradictions and that the intersection of racialization and masculinity was central to these negotiations (Frosh, Phoenix and Pattman 2002).

Boys in the study recognized that gender positioning had changed. They knew from the media and their teachers that girls are doing better educationally than boys, and many complained that their teachers preferred girls or kept telling them that they had to work hard in order to do as well, or better than girls. Most bitterly resented this and also expressed resentment against girls who they reported said things to them like "you're dumb and pathetic". At the same time, many were well aware that, in order to ensure success in the future, they needed to get qualifications. Yet recognizing this could not straightforwardly lead to an engagement with schoolwork because schools are not simply about the gaining of educational qualifications but are equally about negotiating the complex social processes that produce boys' masculine subjectivities.

A pervasive finding in the study was that boys constructed masculinity as being about toughness, style, sporting prowess – particularly at football – and not being seen to get on with schoolwork in the way many girls did. Their subjectivities were produced in relation to each other and to constructions of what masculinities should be like. This did not mean that the boys were cultural dupes who were simply incorporated into already existing gender relations. What it did mean was that they spent a great deal of time negotiating a middle position for themselves in which they could manage what they saw as the demands of masculinities while still getting some schoolwork done, without being "cussed" too much by other boys. One of the ways in which boys resisted the pull of this construction was by recognizing that masculinities are about performances. However, they did not talk about performance as if it is the process by which everybody constitutes subjectivities. Instead, they counterposed performance with authenticity – with, for example, many stating that they were authentic in not claiming to be very tough, while other boys were "just pretending". At the same time, they repeatedly performed in ways designed to avoid giving other boys the opportunity to label them as "gay" or "girl" since these were the insults often applied to boys who were considered not to be keeping in line with popular notions of what constitutes masculinity.

So while boys recognized that they were in changing social circumstances, actively negotiated those circumstances and were self-regulating within the social constraints they experienced, they could not see themselves as free and autonomous or as entirely responsible for optimizing their choices and educational chances. That boys are not simply free to make rational choices becomes even clearer if we consider how masculinities and racialization intersect in their everyday practices.

Constructive and Constraining Masculinities

In British schools, there is a strong egalitarian ideology, with young people asserting that "race", gender and social class do not, and should not, matter. The following quotes are drawn from the accounts of white young men in order to demonstrate that racialization is a relational issue, affecting all young people, even if white young people eschew the notion that it has meaning for them (as in the second quote below):

> Interviewer Right: Do you think there is any racism at school or outside school?
> J: I fink there is some at school yeah ...but I don't like to (.) be racist and I fink it's a bad fing.
> Interviewer Right: So what happens then when people are racist?
> J: Well er, well, one time yeah, my friend, this boy, he had a go at my friend and he's a black boy and I started really havin' a go at him 'cos he called him (.), he called him all these names and I started really havin' a go a this boy and like I said don't do that again and he, and then he hasn't done it before.
> (White 12 year old)

> Interviewer: Do you see yourself as white... Do you think of yourself as being white at all?
> Tony: Not really. I just see myself as being another person. [Interviewer Right] Just someone else. Don't really say like "Oh you're white or you're (.) I'm white, you're black, I'm not gonna (1) hang around with you", 'cos I just think (2) I'm (1) I'm the same as everybody else so. Yeah.
> (White 13 year old)

> Paul: White an' half-caste an' blacks, they're just (inaudible) in the school. They're all friends with white people an' that.
> Interviewer Right: Right. Doesn't matter. What race they are.
> (White 11 year old)

Yet, this apparently rosy story of happy multicultures is contradicted by evidence that there is a great deal of informal segregation in British schools – something that features in young people's accounts:

> Norman: I think there's quite a bit of mixing. [Interviewer Yeah] "Cos um, I've got friends who are black, white, I've got Oriental friends, Asian friends. [Interviewer: Yeah, yeah] I mean there (.) there are groups of people of a particular skin color who (1) who hang around together. Like could be inaudible. It could be understanding, something like that. And um (1) so often a lot of Asian people hang around together in sort of gangs.
> (White 13 year old)

> David: Umm (2) Er (1) yeah, yeah. Because um, some are all (.) the people like, who are black or Asian, they usually (.) the black people, they're usually um (.) they're friends with each other. ...and then the Asian people (1) they're friends with each other. But I'm friends with, I'm friends with basically nearly everyone in the class.
> (White 11 year old)

> Interviewer: You've spoken quite critically about Turkish boys and Somali boys I wonder if ...people did sort of admire them a little bit?
> M: (Wouldn't have thought so) 'cos hardly any (.) they have to hang around with the like (.) Turkish people, have to hang around with the Turkish people 'cos (.) no one hardly likes them. [Interviewer: Right] But if (.) if the Turkish people like stopped being

> aggravating an' that and they tried to speak more English probably like 'em more 'cos we can understand them and get to know 'em. [Interviewer: mmm] But (.) they just talk in Turkish so we can't understand 'em. *slight laugh*
> (White, 14 year old boy)

It is also the case that racism is easily evoked within the school context because, despite the pervasiveness of the egalitarian ideology, it is salient. The following quote from Norman constructs racism as natural and inevitable "as long as there are different races…":

> Norman: I think in the school (.) most (1) most races mix. [Interviewer: Yeah, yeah] I mean occasionally there's a bit of hostility (1) about skin color (1) but (.) there always will be.
> Interviewer: Yeah. Hostility (1) from who to who?
> Norman: I mean um (2) say if there's a black person an' a white person in a fight (1) one of them might say "Oh it's only because of my skin color". Just as an excuse. But that's always gonna happen. [Interviewer: Yeah, yeah] Always. Whatever people say "Oh racism's gonna be stamped out". It's not. [Interviewer: Mmm, mmm] As long as there are different races there will be racism.
> (13 year old white young man)

In this racialized context of school, it is not surprising that masculinities are also racialized. There is ample evidence that black young men of African Caribbean descent are viewed in some ways as "super-masculine" (Sewell 1997). They are constructed as possessing the attributes that are perceived by young men as indicative of the most popular forms of masculinity – toughness and authentically male style in talk and dress. As trend-setters, they may be seen as archetypally active consumers, choosing and producing new styles. This positions them in particularly contradictory ways. At one and the same time, they are feared, discriminated against and face high rates of school exclusions because of those features. However, they are also respected, admired and gain power through taking on characteristics which militate against good classroom performance.

From their research in the US context, Majors and Billson (1992) refer to this as "cool pose" – an aggressive assertion of masculinity that allows control, inner strength, stability and confidence in the face of the adverse social, political and economic conditions which many African American men face. "Cool pose" fits many of the characteristics associated with popular masculinity. However, it also imposes costs on those black boys and men who cannot deal with it simply as performance, but want others to believe that they "really" possess it. What this means is that rather than "playing" with a set of identities which might be adaptable to different contexts, many

Constructive and Constraining Masculinities

black young men find themselves constrained within a construction of masculinity that gives them power in their local situations. However, it contributes to their relative lack of power in society as a whole. Moreover, those boys who attempt to inhabit this prescriptive cultural construction of masculine positions but are "unsuccessful" in doing so, have to deal with failing to achieve racialized, gendered, cultural practices which many have essentialized as natural to black boys.

Schools are racialized and racializing places in that there is, for example, a great deal of informal racialized segregation. In that context, it is not surprising that white masculinities are racialized in relation to black masculinities. Indeed, the pervasiveness of racialized constructions of difference indicates its centrality to the production of identity positions. In the following quotations, hierarchical distinctions are made between Asian, black and white boys.

> Des: Don't know it's just ( ) black boys seem to get friends easier (.) and they're more popular I suppose.
> Interviewer: ...What about in your class, are Asian boys as popular as black boys?
> Des: No I shouldn't think so
> Jason: No
> Interviewer: They're not no
> Des: No (2)
> Interviewer: Why's that? (3)
> Des: Don't really know *sigh* (3) black boys um Asian boys just go round with (.) like who they want (.) but they don't they don't go out picking, they wait for them come to them (1) they've only got a few friends (2) /.../
> (Group interview with 12 year old white boys)

> Interviewer: So ... you're more likely to go around with black boys than Asian boys are you?
> Graham: Yeah
> Interviewer: Why is that do you think?
> Graham: Probably cos like (.) sometimes you think not (.) you ain't you're not really popular an' (.) you know someone who is popular and you go and like try and hang around with them?
> (Group interview with 4 white boys from year 8, 12-13 year olds)

> Interviewer: So they tend to be more interested in football then?
> David: Well, black people are good at athletics, they're very good at running and everything and high jump.
> (11 year old white boy)

The racialization of those cultural practices that define popular masculinities apparently places them out of the reach of white boys, and particularly out of the reach of Asian boys who are constructed by white and black boys as not properly masculine. Some white boys produced narratives that indicated that other white boys wanted to be black, but this was not something they generally claimed that they themselves wanted to be.

> Interviewer: D'you think some white boys then envy black boys (1) 'cos they think they're stronger?
> Paul: Yeah like, they wanna like, some people wanna be black 'cos (1) they might like be more popular. Like, black people like, don't like really cool. Black people have like black slang don't they an' they call people (.) bro an' that (hands). Like white people don't call each other (.) names like that an' black people call some people some. And sometimes people wanna be black an' that./.../
> Interviewer: Yeah, yeah. What about you?
> Paul: I'm not really bothered what color I am. Happy the way (how I'm made). I don't really mind.
> (11 year old white boy)

To some extent, the racialization of masculinities defines black boys outside "normality" since such an envied positioning leads some young white men and teachers to treat young black men as if they are "Other" and "too hard". Young people from all racialized groupings gave accounts that suggest that teachers treat black boys particularly badly. In the second quote below, Lance suggests that he gained instrumental benefits from his teacher's discriminatory treatment in that he did not like the subject from which he was excluded. However, it takes little imagination to recognize that his acquiescence here is likely to damage the qualifications he is able to obtain and, hence, his future life chances.

> Black girl: ...There's this black boy in my class and there's this other white boy, they're always, like, like they're always in trouble together. The both of them and one of them was allowed to go on a trip, the other wasn't and this one who wasn't was actually black you- know. I don't know why that is cos that's sexism and racism...
> White girl: There's a group, yeah in our class and um they don't do anything and it's like black boys and white boys and some half castes and there's um one black boy in it and um like they all do the same things, but he's the one who's been threatened to be expelled and stuff, but no-one else has. /.../
> Black boy: ... Like there's a new teacher who's just come in, Miss --- my form tutor and I always get in trouble even though I don't do nothing. It's like I go to pick up my bag and she says "sit back in your seat" and when somebody else is talking, I get in trouble for it (Right). Cos I know she doesn't like me, cos once, there was me and there was another boy and we both didn't hand in our homework and she gave me a detention and the boy said he lost it and she believed him, so he was allowed to hand his homework in tomorrow, but I got a detention and I handed mine in tomorrow as well.
> (Mixed group -private school)
> Interviewer Right: (2) Do you think some teachers are racist
> Lance: Yeah. Cos like there's sort of like a stereotype for like that black people are feisty....
> Interviewer: So do you think (.) has there been cases where you've been in conflict with a teacher and you think the teacher has been wrong?
> Lance: Last week (1) this teacher gave me a detention for like for absolutely nothing, like, if everyone in the class had said to him that I hadn't, I wasn't talking, cos I was sitting by myself, [Interviewer Mm] anyway, like he still gave me detention okay, and I said, and I said, and because I was arguing about why I was, why I should have a detention then I had to go see the deputy head and I got taken out of like French for the rest of the term, that's alright cos I don't like French.

Constructive and Constraining Masculinities

(14-year-old black young man)

The following account suggests that, for white boys, one reaction to the racialization of masculinities is to construct black boys as other. The quote demonstrates the complex feelings of hate, envy and desire that can be produced through the contradictory positioning of being in the more powerful racialized group in society generally, while being racialized outside powerful masculinity in the school context.

> Interviewer: Why do you think it is that bullies tend to be black boys?
> A: Seems to be all black boys have a chip on their shoulder, you do get white bullies – I'm not sayin' that, but half of the school here, erm, half the black boys - all of them - walk around walkin' like that, brand names, lookin' down at people, like Year Seven's, the little girls. They look at you and stare at you as if you're lower then dem. /.../And they're lookin' at you as if to say, "What you doin' here? Why are you here?" [Interviewer Mmm] Not being racist, but they come over here. Mean I have no problem with black people. Most of my friends are colored and foreign but sometimes it really annoys me especially when they say, "What are you doin' - why are you here? Go home" and all of this. I'm like, I am home, this is England. And I say in my mind, why have I got to go home - I live here. This is my home. Sometimes I feel like sayin' "Go back to your home, Jamaica" -somewhere like that and then think about sayin' most of my friends are colored, be upsettin' them as well./.../ I think about what my friends would feel. I mean the amount of trouble I'd get in. [Interviewer   Mmm] And I realize it would be out of order to say that anyway - it would be racist. [Interviewer Mmm] And that's the last thing I want to be called - racist. [Interviewer Right, ok]
> (12 year old white boy)

The contradictions inherent in the racialization of masculinity makes contestation about masculinities and differential positioning an important aspect of subjectivities for young men – despite the fact that some young men's accounts nuance this racialization rather than making general claims about black, white or Asian boys and young men. There are, however, instrumental benefits for black boys in maintaining their positions as hegemonic in relation to masculinity as in the following quote.

> Interviewer: How important is being black for you?
> Greg: Mm mmm. (1) I don't get picked as I don't get picked on as much as other boys that ain't the same colour as me.
> (11 year old black boy)

It is partly for this reason that many boys (black and white) gave accounts that indicated that black boys often do not welcome white boys' attempts to copy them.

> G: I think I think that because say because I'm white (.) I mean I'm not English or anything but because I'm white they expect me to listen to (.) I don't know (.) Oasis, Blur (*inaudible*) but really but when I was in America so long (.) I've got used to listening to (.) rap, hip-hop S R and B.
> B: Yes and then because he listens to hip hop black people think he's trying to take away what he likes, he likes hip hop (G: They think I'm trying to take away their music) and

89

black people think it's (M: I like *starts mimicking African singer*) just theirs and not his and everyone likes stuff like that but I don't really listen to that I listen to Celine Dion.
Interviewer: So do d'you get criticized then by black people (G Yes yes I do very much) for trying to be black yeah?
G: Yes but but that's only because (.) that's only because I lived in America so long
Interviewer: How do you get criticized...? [T Disses you]
G: Uh you're you're trying to be you're trying to be black you're taking the mick you're taking the piss and all this
M: And you're just a white man
G: You you're just white you're just white trash
Interviewer: Does that happen to you (.) then?
M: Yeah even though I am (.) part of their culture
(White group all year nine, 13-14 years old)

Interviewer: Right. Do you think that there are differences between black, white and Asian boys.
D: Not in color, but what they like, like different songs and stuff like that./.../
D: Yeah, different teams, different footwear - say like I like Reebok
Interviewer: Mmm
D: And black people like Nike and stuff like. I know some white people like Nike as well, and some black people like Reebok, like Darren an Nelson's bruver, 'e likes Reebok...
D: So like I don't mind what they like or what they don't like
Interviewer: (2) Yeah. So what happens if white boys wear the same kind of things that black boys wear?
D: Erm (.) you get the occasion, where the black person who's goin, "Oh, you're trying to act like us, you're tryin to act like us" and sayin "You shouldn't be wearin that coz you're white" but that's bein racist. But all my friends round my area, dey don't what I wear. I've had a pair of Nike trainers before. And dey didn't mind - dey said, "Oh, dey're nice"... And I say, "Fanks", and all 'at.
Interviewer: (.) Were you trying to black, then, by doing that?
D: Nah - I was just wearin dem because it was the latest trend around.
(12 year old white boy)

Greg: Some white boys that hang around with black boys (.) [Interviewer: Right] and like they act like black boys... In like (.) this boy in my class (.) he's white but he tries to act like a black lad (.)
Interviewer: Yeah. W-what do you think of him?
Greg: Mm (2) I think he's stupid a bit...(.) because he tries to bop too much (.) [Interviewer Yeah] an he thinks he's too bad.
Interviewer: What (.) what would (.) you like white boys to be like (.) then?
Greg: Act like white boys act (.) act the way they act not like
Interviewer: How, how do white boys act?
Greg: Not a lot of changes but (.) they should stop trying to (.) speak like black boys cos (.) um, (.) some black and white boys speak differently and (.) they shouldn't try to walk and stuff.
(black, 11 year old)

It is quite clear then that masculinity is a "practical accomplishment" (Connell 1995) that is racialized and struggled over in schools because it incorporates contradictory power relations. Boys' subjectivities are, therefore, constructed from intersections of racialization with gender (as well as sexuality, nation and class). This is a complex and

Constructive and Constraining Masculinities

difficult task. Racialization (like gender) is both a resource in the construction of masculinities and is produced in boys' everyday practices of contestation or conformity. It is marked by anxieties and contradictions – for example, for black boys, between being relatively powerful in locally situated interactions in schools, but not more widely in society. For black boys, these contradictions could mean that they recognized that their behavior was likely to have an adverse impact on their chances of gaining educational qualifications, without being able to easily do anything about it (a dilemma also faced by white boys as they tried to negotiate masculinity). From the account below, it seems that only boys who could still achieve examination success while actively demonstrating that they choose not to engage with schoolwork or comply with expected behavior stand a chance of doing well educationally.

> Interviewer: You mentioned also that that when you first came that quite a lot of of black boys um thought this was a racist school [Greg: yeah] and and um that they were quite lippy.
> Greg: Yeah. Um black boys are probably one of da worst behavin' in this school... Yeah. They like pickin' on white boys that look like - They call them geeks and fings like that
> Interviewer: Right. Why do they do that?
> Greg: Because like if you're in a class um with a lot of black boys an; you're white an like an like you answer all the questions ... they'll start calling you teacher's pet, geek and things like that.
> Interviewer: Why is it that it's mainly white boys that are teachers' pets?
> Greg: Um. Cos cos most black boys in this school. Yeah. Most of them are really bad and they don' really like their subject. They bunk (.) classes and fings like dat.
> Interviewer: Why do you think that is?
> Greg: I don't know. Um (.) probably they wanna show their friends that they're big or something. Because there's like this boy in year eleven he's, um he like he like finks he's big. He's really brainy. When it comes to exams he'll pass all his exams but but he don' like going to lessons and things like that because he wants to show his friends that he's really big.
> (11 year old black boy)

Conclusion

This paper has argued that British society is marked by contradictions between multiethnicity and multiracisms - - contradictions that are evident within the education system, both in terms of the qualifications children obtain and the everyday practices common in schools. The racialization of popular masculinities in schools apparently places them out of the reach of white boys and particularly Asian boys while defining black boys outside "normality" and so opening them to treatment as "Other" and "too hard" by teachers and white boys.

Racialization makes contestation about masculinities and differential positioning an important aspect of boys' subjectivities. This contestation demonstrates that masculinity is a "practical accomplishment" (Connell 1995) that is racialized and where power relations are evident and contradictory. Racialization is thus both a resource in the construction of masculinities and is produced in boys' everyday practices of contestation or conformity. As such, it undoubtedly contributes to anxieties and contradictions for boys. Black boys, for example, are relatively powerful in locally situated interactions, but not more widely, while the opposite situation holds for white boys.

Understanding the challenges inherent in achieving racialized and gendered equality in schools thus requires that we consider the reasons that boys are not entirely free to choose to behave in ways likely to improve their future educational attainment. These reasons center on boys' concern to manage the present rather than the future in the context of complicated, multiple positioning that means that boys are competing with each other just to be accepted as sufficiently masculine.

Works Cited

Cohen, P. "Perversions of Inheritance: Studies in the Making of Multi-Racist Britain." *Multi-Racist Britain*. Ed. P. Cohen and H. Bains. London: Macmillan, 1988.

Connell, R. *Masculinities*. Cambridge: Polity, 1995.

Connolly, P. *Racism, Gender Identities and Young Children*. London: Routledge, 1998.

Frosh, S., A. Phoenix, and R. Pattman. *Young Masculinities: Understanding Boys in Contemporary Society*. London: Palgrave, 2002.

Gillborn, D. *"Race", Ethnicity and Education: Teaching and Learning in Multiethnic Schools*. London: Unwin Hyman, 1990.

---. *Racism and Antiracism in Real Schools*. Buckingham: Open UP, 1995.

Gillborn, D., and C. Gipps. *Recent Research on the Achievements of Ethnic Minority Pupils*. Report for Ofsted. London: HMSO, 1996.

Gillborn, D., and H. S. Mirza. *Educational Inequaltity: Mapping Race, Class and Gender. A Synthesis of Evidence*. London: Ofsted, 2000.

Griffin, C. *Typical Girls?* London: Routledge Kegan Paul, 1985.

Hurrell, P. "Do Teachers Discriminate? Reactions to Pupil Behaviour in Four Comprehensive Schools". *Sociology* 29 (1) (1995): 59-72.

Lees, Sue. *Losing Out: Sexuality and Adolescent Girls*. London: Hutchinson, 1986.

Leonard, M. *Britain™: Renewing Our Identity*. London: Demos and Design Council, 1997.

Mac an Ghaill, M. *Young, Gifted and Black*. Milton Keynes: Open UP, 1988.

Majors, R., and J. Billson. *Cool Pose: The Dilemmas of Black Manhood in America*. New York: Lexington, 1992.

Mortimore, P., C. Owen, and A. Phoenix. "Higher Educational Qualifications." *Ethnicity in the 1991 Census. Volume Four: Employment, Education and Housing among the Ethnic Minority Populations of Britain*. Ed. Valerie Karn. London: Stationery Office, 1997.

Nehaul, K. *The Schooling of Children of Caribbean Heritage*. Stoke-on-Trent: Trentham, 1996.

Ofsted. *Exclusions from Secondary Schools*. London: OFSTED, 1996.

---. *Raising the Attainment of Ethnic Minority Pupil: School and LEA Responses*. London: OFSTED, 1999.

Ogilvy, C., E. Boath, W. Cheyne, G. Jahoda, and H. R. Schaffer. "Staff Attitudes and Perceptions in Multi-Cultural Nursery Schools." *Early Child Development and Care* 64 (1990): 1-13.

Ogilvy, C., E. Boath, W. Cheyne, G. Jahoda and H. R. Schaffer. "Staff-Child Interaction Styles in Multi-Ethnic Nursery Schools." *British Journal of Developmental Psychology* 10 (1992): 85-97.

Osler, A., C. Street, M. Lall, and K. Vincent. *Not a Problem? Girls and School Exclusion*. London: National Children's Bureau and Joseph Rowntree Foundation, 2002.

Richardson, J. "The Role of Ethnicity as a Predictor of Degree Class at the Open University and Other U.K. Institutions: A Research Note." Unpublished paper: Open University Institute Of Educational Technology Student Research Centre, 2002.

Sewell, T. *Black Masculinities and Schooling: How Black Boys Survive Modern Schooling*. Stoke on Trent: Trentham, 1997.

Sonuga-Barke, E., K. Minocha, E. Taylor, and S. Sandberg. "Inter-Ethnic Bias in Teachers' Ratings of Childhood Hyperactivity." *British Journal of Developmental Psychology* 11 (1993): 187-200.

Wright, Cecile. *Race Relations in the Primary School*. London: Fulton, 1992.

Youth Groups and the Politics of Time and Space[1]
Nora Räthzel

While writing the first draft of this paper, pictures of the violence the Italian police was exercising against those demonstrating against the IMF in Genoa haunted me. The television showed stains of spilled blood on the floors and walls of a hall in which the protesters had been sleeping. Then, almost a year after the event, court proceedings confirmed what the protesters claimed: that they had been framed by the police. Policemen first planted the weapons which they then allegedly found in the protestors' dormitories.

Our study was completed almost three years ago. Where would the young people who engaged in street violence at the time of our research stand in such confrontations today? Would they belong to those police forces celebrating the death of a demonstrator they shot? Would they be members of the pink block or of the black block? Or would they belong to the onlookers shaking their heads in disbelief about this group or the other? I do not know. The young people described here have moved on in some direction. Yet the conditions under which they grew up are still there and experienced by others.

Youth gangs like the one which is the subject of this paper have existed for centuries and will continue to exist. The scenery of the spilled blood of protesters provides a good background for understanding their lives. It reminds us not to think of violence as practiced only by those positioned at the margins of society, but to see it first as a means used by institutions of the state against those it considers to be the enemies of its reign. Before any of the young people in our sample were born, the violent dimension of state power was already in place. They grew up knowing about it, fearing it or wishing for its protection.

The data for this article were collected between 1996 and 1999. We were eight people, sociologists, students of sociology and linguistics, social workers, and youth workers, following 160 boys and girls between the ages of 13 and 15 in two neighborhoods of a major German town, Maincity.[2] The young people came from all the different school types the German system has to offer for this age group: secondary school, comprehensive school, and grammar school. While the majority of the young people were born in Germany, their parents were born in 13 different countries, including Germany. They worked as schoolteachers, skilled and unskilled blue-collar workers, skilled and unskilled office workers, cleaners, or were unemployed. A parallel project was conducted with 120 young people in London (see Cohen, Back, Keith 1999). The same methods were used in both cities to get to know the young people, their everyday lives, the relations they developed with each other across ethnic, gender, and class divisions; in addition the peculiarities of the neighborhoods they lived in were taken into account.[3] These were our methods, designed mainly by our colleagues in London:

- *Fashion parade*: Participants were presented with 40 images of youth styles (20 of young women and 20 of young men) which where also differently ethnicized, and asked to pick and comment on three images that they liked and three they disliked.
- *Photoscapes*: Young people were given disposable cameras and asked to photograph places which they thought of as safe or dangerous, and places and people they liked or disliked.
- *Photo Storyboards*: Young people were shown a series of specially constructed photographs depicting young people in peer group situations the meanings of which were ambiguous across a range of ethnic and gender relations. Informants were asked to fill in captions and dialogue to explain the scenes.
- *Genogram*: Young people plotted degrees of contact and levels of intimacy with their friends and relatives and on paper represented them spatially and with the help of color codes indicated their emotional relation towards them.
- *Guided Fantasy*: Young people were given a trigger scenario and asked to write a story utilizing aspects of their real and imaginary landscapes.
- *Audio Diaries:* Young people kept a verbal diary over the period of a week documenting whatever they thought was important during that week.
- *Video Walkabouts:* Young people planned and then conducted walks through their neighborhoods, giving the field workers a "guided tour" commentary as they went.
- *Meeting the project members in London and Hamburg.* With a focus group of 22 young people we visited the London group. A year later, a group of seven young Londoners came to Maincity.

- *Follow Up Interviews:* These took the form of individual semi-structured interviews in which we confronted the young people with a preliminary summary of what we had learned from them, asking them to comment on it.

Some results of our work have been published in various articles over the last three years (see Back, Räthzel, and Hieronymus 1999, Räthzel and Hieronymus 2000, Räthzel 1998, 2000a, 2000b, and 2002). In this paper I concentrate on two particular groups of young people in one of the two neighborhoods, which I call Mixville. The groups were special in so far as many of the young people in our sample, as well as the members of the two groups themselves, saw them as "gangs". Though some of the young people in our sample reported to be members of these "gangs", most of the interviews I draw on in the following text were conducted with older group members, who either attended vocational education or had started an apprenticeship.

Shelden, Tracy, and Brown (1997) note that the definitions of what counts as a youth gang are numerous and diverse. However, one of the elements that feature in most of them is the criminality of gangs. This is not surprising, as a great part of the literature is written by criminologists and by sociologists and ethnologists who aim at helping to solve "the problem of the youth gangs" (see list of references). As I am not interested in questions of crime and violence in this article, and as the young people interviewed here were only occasionally involved in violent fights and thefts, I chose to call them youth groups instead of gangs, avoiding the connotation of a criminal group.

Two classic works in urban sociology, William F. Whyte's *Street Corner Society* and Gerald Suttles' The *Social Order of the Slum*, discovered and presented a social order in neighborhoods that were seen as governed by crime and thus lacking any social order. I see my own approach rather in relation to these authors than to focusing on the criminality of youth groups. Yet, my aim in this article is more modest. I will present a few dimensions of the ways in which members of two youth groups presented their lives in the streets, focusing on their perceptions of time and space. While they were in a transitional phase from youth to adulthood, leaving school and entering the labor market, they were trying to hold on to their traditions and their youthful behaviors and old friendships. I will try to explain why this was the case.[4]

Dangerous Places – Dangerous People

I want to start with the way in which the two youth groups are talked about by some young people in our sample:

> Carl: There are always some people standing in front of the school. Recently they have ripped somebody's clothes, they call themselves Jasons, say the teachers.
> Katrin: I don't have much to do with those Jasons. They are my friends as well, but they're not my cup of tea. They are there for you, if somebody needs to be beaten up or something like that. But they are not my kind of thing. Somehow I am not such a violent person.
> Ami: Adan Square, that's the ultimate meeting place, there are so many kids hanging around there. I don't know anybody who would ever go there in the evening, except if you know them. For instance, if I knew somebody who knows them, I'd go there.
> Viky: There are two from Adan Square in our youth center. I don't like them that much, because they think they can achieve something with violence and I hate that. But these two are quite nice.
> Hassan: Adan Square, there are a lot there who are into violence and I'm not. I live there so I pass by and sometimes I play there. But they don't do anything.
> Hamide: On Koray Adan Square you find the Jasons, but you find them also everywhere else, where there is a fight. I find that totally childish, they play the cool ones with their idiotic fights.
> *Int: And what if you come to the square and say, you want to play basketball, would they chase you away?*
> Hamide: No, I don't think so. They'd play with you.

Certainly, the young people on Koray Adan Square are infamous, they are identified with violence. On the other hand, most of those who reject them have contact with some of them or would like to have some. Other young people do no believe the group is dangerous at all:

> Clara: People say there are gangs. For example there are the Jasons, the famous ones, who cause a bit of stress sometimes. But I don't think they're really dangerous. It's not as if they kill anybody, or anything.

The Jasons are associated with a certain square in the neighborhood and often called after it. The same is true for other groups in the area, which are named after the streets and squares on which they spend most of the time: there are the Edisons, from Edison Street, the Kings from Kings Street, and so on. We find this phenomenon described in most writings on youth gangs; the appropriation of places, which are then defended as turfs, is a common feature. The significance of this process in our context lies in the fact that it is specific to the neighborhood of Mixville as opposed to the other neighborhood in our study, called Monoville. There, places were also seen as dangerous because they were occupied by dangerous people. However, these people were always named after their ethnic background. A place was described as dangerous because Turks or Russians had occupied it. People were seen as being inherently dangerous and therefore making places dangerous. In Mixville dangerous places and dangerous people signified each other. People were seen as dangerous if and because they had the habit of hanging out in a certain place. This made the relationship between people and places more fluid, because being dangerous was not inscribed into one's ethnicity but rather related to the places one chose to visit regularly.

Elsewhere (Räthzel 2000a) I have discussed the different ways of perceiving violence in Mixville and Monoville by examining the histories, representations and lived spaces of these two neighborhoods. In the following I will look at the way in which two groups, the Jasons and the Edisons, see their group formation and their relation to the places they occupy.

The Foundation of a Group

> Aylin: I hang out with the Jasons from Koray Adan Square. *Int: And why on that square precisely?* – Because it's so quiet there, we can talk. *Int: Quiet?* (the interviewer is informed by stories like the ones quoted above.) Yes, because everybody comes there, everybody who is in the clique, they live around the square, that's why they hang out there most of the time.

One might have guessed that group members would see themselves differently than they are seen by others, and the contrast is indeed striking. Likewise, the views of the youth workers in two youth centers, called *Spider* and *Workshop* respectively, are in stark contrast to one another and to the images the young people quoted above conveyed of the Jasons. Lisa from *Spider* describes the Jasons as friendly people, who care for others:

> We encourage self-determination and that means that the young people feel responsible towards new people coming to the center. Two French interns were treated well, the young people helped them to find words, they had a lot of understanding for people with language problems. Sure, there are hierarchies, those who have been here longer sometimes send others to fetch something to eat for them. But they do not form a closed group into which they don't let anyone else.

Minnie from *Workshop* does not only think the Jasons are a closed group, she even credits the youth workers from *Spider* with founding them: "We were very surprised that there was suddenly a group called the Jasons, who emerged through *Spider*, because they think it's great if there is a group. And we don't see that as great at all."

The Jasons describe their formation quite differently:

> Zafer: Well, I've known him (pointing at the boy next to him) let's say, for twelve years, him (pointing at someone further away) for five, six years, and it's because, we have known each other for a long time. Before, we did not have such cliques; we were too young for that. And then, it just happened, that we became a clique of people, because we

have known each other so long. When we were together, this was our street, there were our grandmothers, the little ones were there, and the middle ones. We lived closely together and knew each other well, our parents also knew each other. There are not so many new people, that is, people we've gotten to know recently, say during the last year, or the last two years.

The story of the formation of the Edisons is similar:

> Necai: The group was never founded officially. In the middle of 1995 we met at the playing ground in Bosch Street, and then somebody had the idea, that because we all lived in Edison Street, we should call ourselves the Edison gang. But we have known each other since childhood, really a long time. And everybody knows everybody through school and there we have been able to build even a closer relationship. But since ninety-five we are a group, that's how it is.
> Int: And how long have you been a member?
> Necai: Me? Since I was born.

In Zafer's account the transition from an extended family to the youth group appears to be a natural process occurring as a result of coming into a specific age. A similar naturalization is visible in Necai's statement about being a member of the group since he was born. This reference to a common origin determines their future stability: "Once Edison always Edison", declares Aylin.

These stories are reminiscent of the myths recounting the histories of nation-states. A nation-state that cannot claim an existence of at least 1000 years is not taken seriously (see Räthzel 1997) and will not give its dedicated members the sense of a quasi-natural belonging. Only if things will be the same as they have always been, can a sense of security be maintained. It is this desire for something stable, eternal and therefore natural that these stories speak about. The model after which the groups are shaped is the family: "We are all brothers and sisters", says Zafer, "that's how we see each other. Sometimes there are conflicts, but we are really like a family, everything is being solved." This construction of the group as a family (or as the ideal of a family) can be understood as constructing biographical time as a continuous, reliable process. Time flows in a circular way like the seasons in nature. One can count on things repeating themselves periodically. Zafer's story of how his group acquired its name tells us something about his relation to societal time. It talks about a historical continuity that materialized "behind the back" of its actors:

> Zafer: The name came really from my big brother. Here in Mixville, it was, it is like, you don't say the name, you say, 'Hi Jason, how are you doing?' My brother was at the fun-fair and there you can have something printed on your jacket in nice letters. So my brother had Jasons written on his jacket. And then he didn't wear the jacket anymore, and I walked around with it. And one day, the Koray Adan people wanted to change their name, because it doesn't sounded cool anymore and we wanted a new name, searched,

searched, and then someone said, the colleagues said, we should do what I had done, and then I asked my brother, and then we all discussed it, decided, and that's how the name Jasons came.
And the Jasons, they existed before, about twenty years ago, and the clique was, they weren't so many people, about ten, twenty people, and they used crime, robbery, and all. And then they were grabbed by the police, and they had to dissolve the group, because, they all had a lot of problems. We didn't know that such a group existed as early as twenty years ago, when we started our group. We learned that later from those, what do you call them again, yes, those social workers in Spider. They told us that such a thing had already existed and that they thought it was strange, as if we wanted to copy them, but we didn't know that.

It is quite possible that the tradition of greeting each other with "hi, Jason" is a trace, an unknown memory of the older group, which existed not twenty, but ten years before. Zafer tells the story as a way of relating to and distancing his group from that tradition at the same time. "The Jasons existed before" marks the connection made between the present group and the old one. The insistence that they did not know about the group before they decided on their name, allows Zafer to distance his group from the criminal record of the former one, especially in front of the social workers. Yet their story is told in a compassionate tone, to a certain extent from the point of view of the group, or a worried friend, rather than from the point of view of someone condemning their actions. They are described as *having had* a lot of problems. A more critical narrator might have said that they *caused* a lot of problems. Two histories are constructed in the narrative: First, the recent history of the group Zafer belongs to. It shows him and the other group members as active inventors of a name, and therefore of an identity of the group. Although he describes himself as having an important role in the name-giving, he is more interested in representing the process as democratic: everybody has a say. Asking Zafer's brother also indicates that they respect the original "ownership" of the name. The old history of that other, dangerous group, of which they learned from the social workers, gives their own creativity and inventiveness an additional dignity. They have reinvented (if in a different form) an older tradition of youth gangs in the neighborhood.

When their rival group, the Edisons, retell the story, Zafer's account is reversed and the naming becomes a conscious act of re-naming, of claiming the old group's tradition:

Int: *I have heard that the other group is also called KAS, the abbreviation for Koray Adan Square?*
Cemal: Yes, that was earlier, two years ago, when they wrote KAS everywhere, but now they have called themselves Jasons again. The Jasons have been active before, ten, fifteen years ago, that group already existed. They heard about that.

Historical continuity is constructed on two time-dimensions: individual or biographical time (*we have always been friends*) and societal time (*there have always been youth gangs*). By constructing biographical time as continuous, social relations are at once homogenized and frozen, providing a sense of a secure social network. By constructing societal time as a perpetual reproduction of the same, societal relations are naturalized, whatever happens becomes inevitable, any intervention futile:

> Veli: Yes, one should prevent violence, but how? You can't prevent it. Even if you prevent it today, the little ones, they will certainly do it again, because they become older and older. And then they say, yes, we also want to be like the old ones, one day. Then they'll do it as well.

These images of continuity and reproduction are developed against an experience of the contrary: first, the groups are not as consistent as portrayed by the members. Zafer, who described the Jasons as an extension of his family, did not always belong to the group:

> *Int: Does that mean, you have always been in the clique?*
> Zafer: No, I belonged to another clique. I used to be in my street, in my surroundings, what was closest to me. I was together with my colleagues before, and then we had arguments, and the ones from Koray Adan Square, they are also my friends, so I went to them, as I did not get on with my colleagues anymore.

Cemal from the Edisons has made the opposite move. "I did hang out with the Jasons for a while, but I realized that they were not, how should I put it, well, they were not the right friends for me. We are very different from them." Katrin, who says she grew up with the Edisons and hangs around with them, distances herself from the Jasons because she thinks they are too violent. But it is precisely this violence she takes advantage of when somebody "needs to be beaten up", as she puts it. Second, not only do members drift from one group into another one, the relations between groups vary as well. For instance, the Edisons describe the Jasons as wanting to be the coolest by doing the most stupid things (an expression to describe violence and petty theft), while they themselves are basically the good ones. At the same time they describe each other as friends who share places like youth centers and help each other against groups from other neighborhoods. Third, though they represent their groups as everlasting communities, they know that their future is doomed:

> Zafer: Really, don't know, it was different before. Before, we did everything together, we went everywhere, we did everything together; no matter if it was fighting, going to the movies, to a disco, we did everything together. It is not like that anymore, because, we have grown older and everyone has their private life now. I am working, the colleague here (pointing at his neighbor) is still in school, and he (pointing at another boy) is doing a preparatory year. Everybody is different, nobody finds the time anymore, so we can be

> all together again, like a family. There is only ever five, six people, who go to the disco, or so. We used to do everything together, *everybody goes their own way now*.
> Necai: We have seen that the Edisons, everybody took care of everybody else. It was like that, only now one has an apprenticeship, the other is getting married soon, this and that and *everybody goes their own way*. But everywhere, where we meet, or we know where to find someone, if we need him, we know the place.

Zafer's continuous repetition of the phrase "we did everything together," indicates his deep worry about the changes that have occurred. It is as if repeating the sentence again and again could bring back those times. Necai's account is more hopeful, he still believes that in spite of their different trajectories the Edisons will still be able to find and support each other. Both accounts include the same expression signifying spatial movement as well as a process, which could be called individualization according to theories of modernization or of a "reflexive modernity". However, to understand the character of this process the concept of privatization seems more adequate. Privatization is commonly used to describe a transition of bodies from public into private ownership. The etymology of the word leads to the Latin word "privare", which means, "to deprive (retaining the Latin root), rob, free". The private man, seen as the free man, is at the same time the man deprived of his social relations.[5] When Zafer says that everybody has a private life now and therefore many do not come to the group any more, he points at this process of deprivation. The young people moving on to jobs and into families lose connection with their former friends and are thus deprived of the common ground that enabled them to support each other. If each one goes his/her own way, their experiences will differ. Following one's own way includes the absence of other marchers on that path, and this excludes the possibility of finding support. Searching for work also means that individuals are positioned against each other as competitors for jobs.

The two boys telling these stories are both seventeen years old. Zafer attends a course that is supposed to prepare him for an apprenticeship while Necai attends a vocational school to become an office worker. They have left the place where most of their friendships were formed, school. Yet they do not want to let go of their old lives. They still frequent the same places they gathered at when they went to school together. At the same time they are aware that not only their friends have changed and started to disappear, the places themselves have changed as well.

> Cemal: A lot of Yugoslavs have come here over the last year, and gypsies and so on, who have been begging in the streets. Of course, that doesn't fit into our neighborhood, to say it bluntly. But, it used not to be that way in the past and I really don't want to accept

changes. I want Mixville to stay as it always is, that we always stay friends and can hang out together every day. But we can't do it every day...

For Cemal Mixville "as it always is" (the use of present tense where the past tense would be appropriate, signifies the transposition of the past into the present and the desire to freeze that state) is synonymous with the place where friends always stay friends. Like his peers with German background, this young man of Turkish descent ascribes threatening changes in the neighborhood to foreigners. His desire for stability is tainted by the knowledge that this stability is doomed, in fact, has already vanished. The only way to preserve it is to dwell in the past, therefore Cemal wants to become a writer: "Later I want to get an education and I would like to become a writer and write a book about us, about the Edison gang, the way we were in the past. I think the book will become a big success."

Necai wants to reshape the past by constructing a different present for people in the future to remember:

> We, that is our street, we were worse before, our older people, our brothers, they were worse. We try to build a generation, where there is a youth gang, of which one used to say, well, they thought for a while that we did only stupid things. We have tried to produce justice but differently, not through discussion, but through violence, so people would understand us. But now, we want to be like... that later, people will say about us that we were good, not bad.

Necai wants to break the tradition of the violent youth gang, to reinvent it through a new presence that will become the group's identity for the future. His aim for continuing the group is therefore also to change it.

That the young people hold on to a past that is rapidly changing suggests that it fulfils a need for them that cannot be fulfilled by other means. Wanting to have friends on whom one can rely in times of need seems reasonable enough. But why do they have to form a group? A first answer that we also find in the literature written on youth gangs (see the overview in Shelden *et al.*) was given above. Zafer mentioned how the Edisons help the Jasons when groups from outside the neighborhood attack them, and Katrin says, "yes, that's the way it is today, young people are that way, they look for trouble, and if you are not in a clique today, you are really lost." This may explain why young people choose to be in youth groups while they are at school and can become the victims of other people their age. However, it does not explain why some of them want to hold on to their group when this threat has vanished because the threatening groups have dissolved. An explanation can be found in Zafer's and Veli's description of their daily lives in the street.

> Veli: We stay on the streets, because after 6 p.m. that's when the day really starts to begin for us again, and then it's cold and we decide, say, to go to the Mall, with five, six people, and when we are sitting at a corner there, the guards come and chase us out, because we …
> Zafer: Yes, and then it's like "the Turks" again, or …
> Veli: Because we stick out.
> Zafer: Because we're foreigners.
> Veli: And then they ban us from the place.
> Zafer: Just because of the way we look, they don't let us in. It's like: "I don't like your face, get out of here." For instance there is that bin, where you can put out your fags. Somebody, a German guy smokes and nobody says anything. A colleague goes there, and it's like: "Come on, put out your cigarette and get out. You're banned for today!" "Why?" "You're not allowed to smoke here." And I say, "but there was just somebody smoking." "That's not true, I am sorry, you have to get out." It's not as if it happens all the time, but it happens.
> *Int: Have you done anything to change it?*
> Zafer: We can't do anything because we'll always have the poor hand. If we don't do anything, we're back on the street, if we do something, then the police will be there in a minute: "Oh yes, we know you, you've been here before, come with me."
> Veli: We have no chance. We just want to be left alone. When we show up, they think we want to turn the whole place upside down. We're constantly observed. They're afraid of young people. They think we are all the same.
> Zafer: They have no idea how we really are. They cannot say we're all the same, they can't say we're all assholes; they can't say we're all good.

The way in which the two boys pick up each other's sentence and continue them transmits the sense of a story that has been experienced and told many times. There are different ways of interpreting this passage. As the boys expect the police to take them away because they know them to disturb the order, the passage can be read as a form of self-victimization, a way of seeking pity from the interviewer and from adults in general. At the same time we know from the literature (see for instance Tizard and Phoenix 1993) and from numerous accounts that black and migrant youth are subject to more surveillance, and stopped more often by the police than their white and non-migrant peers. No matter whether the boys here have contributed to the way they are perceived, what counts for them is that they are treated as suspicious irrespective of what they do. As the guards cannot possibly know whether they are good or not, it would not make any difference if they were. They would still face the same problems; they would still not have a place to go where they would be accepted.

In one of the video walkabouts two girls with German background told us how they used the mall. They went to the roof and observed the people using the sauna in the neighboring building. It was forbidden to go to the roof, and the girls were thrown out sometimes. But for them this was a sport. They tried to see how long they could stay without being found. No matter how often they were thrown out, they were never banned.

For the guards and for the police, the non-native boys, especially those with a Turkish background, are the ones who occupy the subject position of the troublemakers in Mixville. Therefore, the trouble caused by boys and girls with a German background is perceived as the normal nonsense young people their age are bound to do. The same behavior coming from young people with a migrant background evokes images of dangerous youth who must be stopped from the outset. Even when German boys become members of a youth group considered as a gang, they are not seen as occupying the same position as the migrant boys and girls within that group. The social worker, who was keen to dissolve the Edison group in order to transform them into decent boys, only had a dismissive remark for German boys joining gangs: "They probably only do it because they are afraid of the gangs." While this could be the case for some boys, as a statement about German boys in general, it assumes that there is an inherent difference between young migrants forming or joining groups and young native Germans doing so.

Unchanging Places, Cyclic Time and the Question of Marginalization
We can now begin to make a connection between the everyday life of these groups of young people and their desire for the security that unchanging places and circular time provide. I would like to suggest that this desire to hold on to a naturalized peer group and to an unchanging place, as well as the belief that time keeps repeating itself, is engendered by experiences of marginalization and discrimination. By going into the shopping mall they make the transition from the public streets of their neighborhoods to the private space of the mall. On a local level they transcend the appropriated space of their childhood to step into the privatized space of capital, the space that awaits them when they begin working. In that sense, the behavior of the guards and the police is a symbol for what they can expect once they leave their neighborhood – and they know this:

> Necai: Well, we are satisfied with Mixville, happy. ... In Mixville I know, if I look backwards somebody else is going to give me cover, somebody will take care of me, but when I am outside Mixville, I know I am totally alone and I get anxious and nervous.

One of the things Necai is afraid of when he leaves Mixville is to be attacked by skinheads as once happened to him and his friend while riding the metro. This anxiety is

Youth Groups and the Politics of Time and Space

augmented by his fear of the police. He did not report the attack to the police because he does not want to have anything to do with these authorities. Cemal describes the security that Mixville provides in opposition to the rest of the city:

> We are lucky living in Mixville, because outside, in the city, there are a lot more Germans, and there are a lot more people who dislike foreigners, but here in Mixville, most of the Turks and foreigners live here.

In fact only 35 % of the population of Mixville has a migrant background.

As the young men feel that they do not have any place outside Mixville, it is difficult for them to shift their local belonging to a more general level of national or class belonging. Likewise, to belong to one of the lifestyle-groups, which, as some recent theories about youth suggest, have replaced class and national belonging, seems impossible. This is not because they do not belong to such groups. With their preference for name brand clothes and hip hop they certainly form part of a particular lifestyle. Equally, their parents' social position and their own work aspirations make them members of specific strata of the working class. However, no matter how much they fit into any of these social groups, first and foremost they will be seen as "foreigners" and treated accordingly.

In Mixville they have been able to create a place they can consider their own, a place that belongs to them and where they belong. They believe (and they may be right) that they have created this place partly through the use of violence. They have not experienced serious racial harassment, they say, "because in Mixville everybody is afraid of us." In addition, Mixville provides a home for them because it is a place that accommodates difference. Zafer formulates that well:

> If you look at those chains of shops, the Turk starts there, and there the Albanian ends. And where the Albanian ends, the Yugoslav starts with his shop. And I mean, living together here, if we would look at Greece or Turkey and then here, where the Turks end, you see Greeks and they are fully satisfied with it. I am also learning Greek.

The diverse ethnicities which comprise their groups are seen as an asset, enabling the young people to learn from each other:

> Necai: Colleagues of mine, a German and a Yugoslav, they came every day and they decided to learn Turkish. I thought that's impossible but when you hear them now, you'd say that is not a German, not a Yugoslav, his Turkish is perfect. ... And if a Yugoslav takes me to his parties and I can learn something about his culture, I think that's great. As long as he accepts me, I can accept him.

In Mixville, diversity, being a "foreigner", can be seen as the norm. The young people know that this is exceptional for the city they live in and differs from Germany as a whole. The moment each of them follows their own way, the security they have found in being part of an accepted diversity is lost. It will be difficult for them to recreate similar relations of belonging in other places, which are not structured by diversity in the same way. Therefore, they cannot (or only with great difficulty) accompany the process of privatization, of being deprived of social relations structured through mutual trust and respect, by a process of individualization, of becoming unique and independent individuals. Most discussions about the ever-increasing individualization in postmodernity do not take into account that there are people to whom individualization (in the sense of becoming independent and unique) is denied. The young people presented here are perceived not as individuals in their own right, but as representatives of a type. They are already known and judged before they act. It is not too much individualization that is their problem, but the impossibility to individualize. "They think we're all the same," Zafer said.

In Mixville they are able to counter this portrayal of themselves: Being members of youth groups provides them with a sense of commonality, of sameness in relation to the members of their own group, but at the same time it also gives them a sense of being unique. They differ from other groups in terms of the squares or streets they occupy, and the activities they engage in. These activities enable them to develop their self-esteem by protecting themselves from being put down. As Zafer and Cemal remark: "Normally we are not harassed that much in the streets, 'cause if people see there are five or six Turks, they think immediately, better not to say anything, they are going to slap us in the face." It seems difficult to convince young people of the virtues of non-violent behavior, when they experience that it is precisely the image of being violent that earns them respect, or at least protects them against racist behavior. That there is some truth in their judgment of the situation may be assumed by the fact that girls of migrant background (in and outside of youth groups) reported a number of incidents where they have been called names and harassed in the streets.

In his lectures on Shakespeare Auden, analyzing Iago, the character in Shakespeare's *Othello* who acts evil just for the fun of it, suggests that the only way for a man to be free is to reject necessity: "... his ego seeks constantly to assert its autonomy by doing something of which the requiredness is not given, something which is completely arbitrary, a pure act of choice." Such an act can be defined as an *acte gratuit*, like the one of an artist, of players who make their own rules or, of a criminal: "... a man asserts his freedom by disobeying a law and retains a sense of self-importance because the law he has disobeyed is an important one, one established either by God or society." (Auden 2000: 198). The boys in the groups presented here certainly feel that they live by their own rules and show a desire for a life of self-determination. Necai gives a vivid account of this desire:

> Once, in 1996, I tried to get a room for us. I wrote a letter to the youth office, which I did not mail, but still I got an appointment with a youth worker. The point was, we were always sitting on that playing ground, and many people complained about us and we were fed up with that and therefore I wanted to apply for a room, for after the time when the *Workshop* is open, until ten p.m. or so. A room where we are all alone, where everybody can do what they want, but has to clean up everything afterwards. We wanted to organize a disco ourselves, but everything went down the drain, because nobody was interested in us. The room was not supposed to be just for the Edison clique, it should be a youth center for everybody. We wanted to act as social workers ourselves, and we wanted to do everything they do in a youth center, but just without anybody telling us what to do. And they told us, yes, yes, but in the end nothing came of it. And therefore, I want to especially thank you (directed towards the interviewer) for coming here, for seeking contact with us, for showing an interest in who we are. Because many of us see that as an opportunity to talk, to really say what we think.

Who knows, a self-organized youth center might not have been viable. It might have ended in destroyed furniture and violent fights between different groups claiming access. Nevertheless, it would have been worth trying, especially as violence and destruction occur in official centers as well.[6] What is important here is that the result of Necai's efforts contributed to his and his friends' conviction that nobody trusts them and that nobody cares about them. His story is marked by a contradiction: On the one hand, it speaks of the strong desire for independence and self-determination, on the other, it is a plea for care, for having people take an interest in them. A similar desire is articulated by Zafer and Veli, when the interviewer asked them how they would like to be treated. Zafer: "They should take care of us." Veli: "They should not see us as foreigners but as human beings, as people". Zafer: "Like any other normal human being, any normal one."

Wanting to be normal provides another clue to the group's sometimes violent actions and the stealing of brand name clothes: They can be interpreted as an attempt to become just the sort of young people society wants them to be – oriented towards upward mobility, following the latest fashion to satisfy the brand's need for profits. The young people are, in a way, tragic heroes: The more they try to become normal through the only resources they have, the more they are bound to resemble the picture they want to escape – a bunch of dangerous foreigners.

A number of theories concerned with youth gangs and youth criminality suggest that young people become delinquent because they learn criminal behavior from adults, because there is a gap between the expectations society produces and their resources to realize them, because they lack the appropriate male role-models at home, or because they reject middle-class values and acquire working-class values instead, which include a certain kind of masculinity marked by "toughness" and "smartness" (Goldstein 1991; Cloward and Olin 1960; Miller 1958; Johnstone 1983; Hagan 1993).

The youth groups presented here tell a different story. The values they learn do not differ decisively from the middle-class norms they are taught in school. What is different is the way in which these norms are applied to them. If they experience discrimination by the same authorities that represent the values they are asked to follow, how are they supposed to take them seriously? If they are reduced to their ethnic background, and can only find respect through being feared, how are they supposed to believe in the values of equality based on a universal humanity? As Willis once wrote about the lads, it is not a lack of knowledge that drives young people to become what they are seen to be; it is their insight (however partial) into the ways in which society works to exclude them that motivates their actions (Willis 1977,126 ff). Through their experiences, these young people are bound to transgress the surface of respectable values and find themselves amidst the machinery of a quite different, unjust society. One way of surviving is to play according to the rules that are at work instead of believing in those they are taught.

Appropriation of Space or Appropriated by Space? The Dialectics of Agency and Subordination

Zygmunt Bauman has examined the different modes of space and time those who can take advantage of postmodern times and those who cannot experience:

> For the first world, the world of the globally mobile, the space has lost its constraining quality and is easily traversed in both its 'real' and 'virtual' renditions. For the second world, the world of the 'locally tied', of those barred from moving and thus bound to bear passively whatever change may be visited on the locality they are tied to, the real space is fast closing up. ... People marooned in the opposite world are crushed under the burden of abundant, redundant and useless time they have nothing to fill with. In their time 'nothing ever happens'. They do not 'control' time-but neither are they controlled by it, unlike their clocking-in, clocking-out ancestors, subject to the faceless rhythm of factory time. They can only kill time, as they are slowly killed by it. (1998, 88).

The young people in our sample seem to fit perfectly into this description: Their space certainly closes up and they have an abundance of time:

> Zafer: We don't really do much, we smoke, everyone talks about their problems, we talk a lot among us, we do things, we make plans but if an important person can't come, we leave it or we do it all the same. We just pass the time.

Yet on another level they do make an effort to control time (if not the actual daily hours); they try to fix and contain it in their stories about everlasting friendships and the circular reproduction of events. They do not "bear passively" what happens to their local space. They have actively appropriated places and are engaged in a number of activities in order to preserve them. Ironically, it is the moment of transition, the moment they are meant to go beyond the borders that have surrounded their adolescent lives, when their actions freeze and turn against them. The places they have appropriated seem to have taken hold of them. What was their strength – to root themselves in their neighborhood – turns into their weakness once the conditions for this kind of rooting begin to disappear. In retrospect, it may seem as if, instead of appropriating places, they have been appropriated by them, reproducing the spatial marginalization society had designated for them. The place that belongs to them and to which they belong is the place they are relegated to by the exclusionary practices of society at large.

However, their story does not end here, there remains the other side of the coin. In appropriating these spaces, the young people have also developed their creativity, their social skills and their capacity for solidarity. Even if Necai's attempt to set up an independent youth center failed, it has provided him and his friends with knowledge about state institutions: The ideas and insights formulated by him and Zafer, Veli and Cemal show them clinging to their old ways but also expressing hopes and plans for the future. With the resources they have acquired in shaping their local places, and being shaped by the possibilities its diversity had to offer, they might eventually be able to move on and recreate new, flexible places of belonging.

Endnotes

[1] A short version of this text appeared in *Soundings*, Issue 23, Autumn 2003.

[2] I have changed the names of places and people to protect the anonymity of the respondents.

[3] The Volkswagenstiftung funded the German part of the research and the ESRC the British part.

[4] I would like to thank Gabriela Mischkowski, Yael Feiler, and Angelika Magiros for reading an earlier draft and making very useful comments in spite of their own busy schedules.

[5] I use the male form deliberately, since the construction of the free private man excludes women.

[6] In his study " Street Corner Society" Whyte reports how a youth center managed by a fomer street corner boy of the neighborhood was the only one of three opened at the same time which was successful. In spite of this, it was closed down and the young people had attended it were back on the streets together with their manager. It would be interesting to investigate why, with all concern about getting young people off the streets, possibilities that do not imply control are rarely tried.

Works Cited

Auden, W.H. *Lectures on Shakespeare.* London: Faber and Faber, 2000.

Back, L., N. Räthzel, and A. Hieronymus. "Gefährliche Welten – sichere Enklaven. Alltagsleben von Jugendlichen in zwei Hamburger und zwei Londoner Stadtteilen." *Archiv* 2 (1999): 7-62.

Bauman, Zygmunt. *Globalization. The Human Consequences.* London: Polity Press, 1998.

Cloward, R., and L. Ohlin. *Delinquency and Opportunity.* New York: Free Press, 1960.

Cohen, Phil, Michael Keith, and Les Back. *Finding the Way Home: Issues of Theory and Method.* CNER/ CUCR Working papers 6. London: Centre for New Ethnicities Research & Centre for Urban and Community Research. University of East London, 1999.

Goldstein, A. P. *Delinquent Gangs: A Psychological Perspective.* Champaign IL: Research Press, 1991.

Hagan, J. "The Social Embeddedness of Crime and Unemployment." *Criminology* 31 (1993): 465-491.

Johnstone, J.C. "Youth Gangs and Black Suburbs." *Pacific Sociological Review* 24 (1993): 355-373.

Miller, Walter B. "Lower Class Culture as a Generating Milieu of Gang Delinquency." *Journal of Social Issues* 14 (1958): 5-19

Räthzel, N. *Gegenbilder. Nationale Identitäten durch Konstruktionen des Anderen.* Opladen: Leske und Budrich, 1997.

---. "The Usage of Social Space and Ethnic Categories in Interviews with Young People in Hamburg". *Socio-Cultural Problems in the Metropolis: Comparative Analysis.* Eds. Dirk Hoerder and Rainer-Olaf Schultze. Hagen: ISL, 2000a. 37-55.

---. "Living Differences: Ethnicity and Fearless Girls in Public Spaces." *Social Identities* 6, 2 (2000): 119-142.

---. "Antirassistische Moral als Form der Ausgrenzung". *Konjunkturen des Rassismus.* Eds. Alex Demirovic and Manuela Bojadzilev. Münster: Westfälisches Dampfboot, 2002.

---. "Listenreiche Lebensweisen: Der Gebrauch von Ethnizität im Alltag von Hamburger Jugendlichen." *Migration und Soziale Arbeit, Zusammenleben in den Städten* 3-4 (1998): 32-38.

Räthzel, N., and A. Hieronymus. *The Hamburg Story: The Everyday Lives of Young People in a German Metropolis.* Working paper 6. Centre for New Ethnicities Research, University of East London, 2000.

Shelden, Randale G., Sharon K. Tracy, and William B. Brown. *Youth Gangs in American Society.* Belmont: Wadsworth, 1997.

Suttles, G. D. *The Social Order of the Slum.* Chicago: U of Chicago P, 1968.

Tizard, B., and A. Phoenix. *Black, White or Mixed Race? Race and Racism in the Lives of Young People of Mixed Parentage.* London: Routledge, 1993.

Whyte, W. F. *Street Corner Society.* Chicago: The U of Chicago P, 1961.

Willis, P. *Learning to Labour. How Working Class Kids Get Working Class Jobs.* Farnborough, Hants.: Saxon, 1977.

Dynamics of Integration and Segregation: Ethnic Minorities in Germany

Birgit Rommelspacher

Over the past several years there has been an ongoing debate in many countries concerning the question of cultural diversity in an increasingly globalized world. Within each society there are different images or visions of diversity. In the USA for example the traditional image of a melting pot has given way to the notion of a salad bowl. Canadian and British society seem to favor the vision of a mosaic, whereas in the Netherlands the image of different pillars shaping society is more prevalent. All of these images point to the fact that there are also different strategies in dealing with diversity.

In Germany the prevailing image of society is still one of ethnic homogeneity. This has, as will become evident, mainly to do with the historical process of nation building and the difficulties of finding a common ground in the struggle for political unity. This image of homogeneity again is linked to an attitude of paternalism in dealing with minorities, which is important since the question of heterogeneity in a society is always linked to the question of equality and inequality. One could say that there is an interconnection between the "horizontal" dimension of diversity and the "vertical" dimension of hierarchy.

There are marked national variations as to the location of ethnic minorities within the social strata as well as in the degree of social inclusion versus exclusion. On the one hand, this depends on the political culture of the country of immigration and, on the other hand, on the specific relationship between the majority population and the different ethnic minorities. This relationship is mainly shaped by cultural communalities and differences as well as by the different political and economic interests. Against this background I will give a brief overview of the situation of ethnic minorities in Germany and demonstrate how their stance in society is linked to the political culture.

Ethnic Minorities in Germany

Up until the 1960s Germany was first and foremost a country of emigration. For many centuries a high proportion of Germans emigrated. Initially these emigrants headed mainly east to such countries as Russia, Poland or Rumania, whereas in the 18th, 19th and 20th centuries their chief destination was the West, especially the Americas. The legacy of this century long emigration is manifold and has had a profound influence on present-day immigration. This is not only the case with the people who are coming "back" to Germany; it also impacts the national legislation, which has primarily been defined by the *jus sanguinis*, which decrees that only people of German descent are Germans. This is typical for emigration countries since the emigrants were able to retain both their citizenship and the option to return. But although Germany has now become a *de facto* country of immigration, the same legislation has been used as a means to restrict full citizenship rights for immigrants and their children.

However, the greatest impact in the history of German emigration has been the "return" of numerous ethnic Germans, especially since the fall of the wall in 1989. Often these persons of German origin were persecuted in Russia and Poland during and after World War II because of their real or alleged connection with the National Socialist regime. In addition to being discriminated as Germans, the poor economic prospects in these countries have often been the driving force to emigrate to Germany. Consequently, the 3.6 million Russian and Polish-Germans are the largest ethnic minority in Germany today (Münz et al. 1997). Although these ethnic Germans, the so-called "Aussiedler/innen" (re-settlers), do not appear as ethnic minorities in official statistics and are not considered to be immigrants in the public discussion, the majority nevertheless often treats them as such. Often, they are seen mainly as "Ausländer," i.e., as non-Germans. Paradoxically they are accused of being too German, that is more German than the Germans themselves. (Bade 1994, Räthzel 1997, Beger 2000).

Aside from these ethnic Germans there have been diverse groups of people living in Germany from time immemorial, namely the Jews, the Sinti and Roma, the Sorbes and the Danes. Another minority, the Afro-Germans, are of quite different origins. Partly their ancestors were summoned from African countries by kings and emperors. Others came in the aftermath of German colonialism; again others are offspring of African American soldiers stationed in the Federal Republic of Germany after World War II, or the children of African "Vertragsarbeiter" mostly from Angola and Mozambique, who worked as contract laborers in the former German Democratic Republic. And others still are offspring of refugees from various countries in the world.

But the group which nowadays has actually come to symbolize ethnic minorities in Germany are the "guest workers", in particular the Turks. These migrant workers were recruited by West-Germany during the years of accelerated economic growth from the early 1960s until the end of the 1970s. They came from different Mediterranean countries, over the past years predominantly from Turkey. Today, the Turks are the minority at the center of most public discourse – especially since anti-Islamic sentiment has grown steadily during the past two decades. Since the time of the "guest workers" immigration has consisted mostly of refugees, especially from the former Yugoslavia, but also from countries all over the world.

Despite this ethnic heterogeneity Germany until recently practiced a policy of denial and negation: "Germany is not an immigration country" was the dominant slogan of most German politicians throughout the past decades. This denial was twofold: the ethnic Germans are not seen as immigrants because they are not foreigners but Germans, and the "foreigners" are not considered to be immigrants because they are expected to return to their country of origin. As a consequence, there was no meaningful immigration nor integration policy. Only recently has there been a change in federal government policy: a governmental commission was established to draft an immigration law. In a recent report the commission stated that "Germany needs immigration" (Zuwanderungs-Kommission 2001). Yet at the moment it is unclear if this law will ever be passed and, moreover, whether it will really transform German society.

The main question therefore remains why Germany relies so heavily on images of homogeneity and on the notion of a closed society despite its varied history of immigration and emigration. In fact, this has to do primarily with the history of nation building, which was a very difficult process during the 19th century. At that time Germany was divided into hundreds of different political entities (principalities and kingdoms dominated by sovereigns exerting absolute power). Furthermore, it was fragmented by religious strife and conflicting regional interests. The struggle for "unification" was a highly contentious one. The establishment of a nation-state neither embraced all Germans (the Austrians in particular were excluded), nor were all citizens of this new nation Germans, such as the Poles, the Czechs or the Danes. The lack of territorial and political unity was one of the main reasons why the concept of nation was not based on a political vision as for example in France or England but on a predominantly ethnic concept of nation. The less a real basis for this new nation seemed to exist, the more the search for a common ground fostered a looking back into pre-historical times and into mystification. The myth of a common origin and the flight into idealism was thus chiefly due to the lack of communalities, and so the concept of a uniform German national culture emerged.

This seems to be a crucial dimension in the political culture of Germany up to the present day, especially since National Socialism radicalized the concept of ethnicity in an unprecedented manner. Its murderous drive for homogeneity not only led to the expulsion and annihilation of millions of people viewed as "non-Aryan", but in addition these politics led to a disastrous war which forced twelve million ethnic Germans to flee from eastern Europe, entirely changing the character of the population in Germany. Thus, National Socialism turned Germany into a comparatively ethnically homogeneous country. This not only defines the situation in Germany in terms of ethnic homogeneity but has also had a decisive impact on German political culture.

The concept of homogeneity is therefore crucial to understanding the different socio-economic standings of ethnic minorities in Germany. Accordingly, it seems useful to ask how a specific minority relates to what might be called Germanness. Hence one could distinguish between minorities "within" the Germans, those "outside", and finally the "outsiders within".

Minorities *within the Germans* are those forming different "layers of Germanness". The "Germans" in a hegemonic sense are firstly represented by the West Germans, whereas for example the East Germans are not accepted as Germans in the same way. To a certain extent they are considered to be more German than the West Germans, as more traditional, e.g. relying on old Prussian traditions in contrast to a modern, dynamic and internationally oriented Germanness represented by the West Germans. The hegemonic Germanness is characterized by an ambivalent relation to tradition, on the one hand embracing it and on the other distancing oneself from it. In other words, it is the West Germans who define what is supposed to be an acceptable tradition and what should be abandoned. The power to define tradition is an important element of a symbolic power, allowing one to label the "others" as backward and thus as less German. This is not only the case with regard to the East Germans but even more so in terms of the "Aussiedler/innen", the ethnic Germans from eastern European countries. They enjoy certain political privileges compared to other immigrants, since it is easy for them to obtain a German passport as well as receiving financial and social support to facilitate their integration into German society. However, they are even less accepted as

Germans, because they are seen as even more traditional, and their Germanness is often believed to be only a pretext for economic gain.

The term "Ausländer" is directed at all those who are *outsiders* and supposedly do not belong to this country. This term includes not only people without a German passport, i.e., all those who are defined as not being German. It is mostly used in connection with the so-called guest workers, primarily the Turks – less so today for Italians or Portuguese. But also Afro-Germans are seen as foreigners.

Finally, there are the minorities who are *outsiders within*, especially the Jews, who are seen as part of German society but at the same time treated as a "special group". The century old common history, and especially the period of National Socialism, have been decisive in defining the relationship to the Jewish population. Within mainstream German society people feel highly ambivalent towards their Jewish neighbors. On the one hand, Jews are kept at a distance and seen as somehow foreign, on the other hand, an intimate relationship exists since they elicit unpleasant memories of the past. They have become part of the conflicting self-images of the non-Jewish Germans, since they symbolize a past which must be suppressed. The Jews often provoke feelings of guilt because they have been forced into the role of a collective Super-ego. Their voices are heard, in particular in dealing with matters related to the past, while at the same time they feel offended and are envied for having been delegated this moral authority (Bar-On 1995; Rommelspacher 1995).

Although the Sinti and Roma, like the Jews, were also persecuted as a "race" under National Socialism, they do not play the same symbolic role, since they do not elicit similar feelings of guilt as the Jews. This seems to indicate that there is a hierarchy of victims. The racism expressed towards the Sinti and Roma is more widely accepted publicly and can be seen in the light of an unquestioned historical continuity.

Thus the symbolic position as well as the political and socio-economic situation of ethnic minorities in Germany is closely linked to their own history. Again this is very much determined by the political culture, which in Germany is mainly based on images of ethnic purity. Therefore, the integration of ethnic minorities into German society is mainly equated with assimilation. But the concept of assimilation embraces the paradox that people are supposed to submerge into a Germanness to which they have no access. To become German is not possible for those without German ancestors. This claim for something unattainable is one of the chief sources of power of the ethnic majority.

Accusing the "Other" of not being willing or able to assimilate provides the legitimation for a wide range of discriminatory practices. It is, therefore, not surprising to find that German society is deeply divided along ethnic lines.

Segregations in German Society

Segregation is a complex phenomenon and pervades many social dimensions. The dividing line between ethnic minority and majority is especially relevant to political, economic, social and cultural issues. Cultural segregation is nowadays most prominently expressed in the dichotomy between Islamic culture and the Christian or Western culture, which are seen as being basically incompatible. This has been espoused, for example, in several so-called "veil-debates" forbidding Islamic pupils and teachers to wear a veil in public schools. Likewise formidable barriers have been placed on the teaching of Islam in the public schools in contrast to instructions in the Catholic, Protestant or Jewish religions. Anti-Islamic sentiments are prevalent in the symbolic struggle of what is considered to be a modern German society. But this obviously is an international phenomenon and also holds true for countries like France, Britain, the Netherlands or the United States.

The political dimension of segregation, on the other hand, is quite specific to the German situation. In contrast to other countries of the European Union Germany, together with Austria and Switzerland, requires the longest waiting period for immigrants or refugees to obtain the right to unlimited residence, let alone German citizenship. In terms of the former there is a specific set of regulations stipulating that the applicant must have sufficient living space, verification of employment, have made payments into the state pension fund for a minimum of five years and is not allowed to receive any welfare benefits. These regulations do not exist in most other European countries (Davy 2001). For immigrants in Germany this means that they are in for the long haul in terms of attaining legal equality. Without German citizenship they do not have the right to vote, even when they have been living in Germany for several decades.

But recently there has been a change in government policy. A limited dual citizenship has been conferred on children born in Germany; at birth they receive both the German and the parental citizenship. However, when reaching adulthood they have to decide if they want to become Germans or opt for the citizenship of their parents. The political and ideological traditions of Germany make it impossible to accept dual or multiple citizenships, since there seems to exist only an either/or mentality – a thinking in dichotomies. This may also explain why there is no policy of granting periodic amnesty in Germany for undocumented workers as is the case in France, Spain or the USA.

Political segregation makes it difficult for immigrants to identify with German society. A comparative study of immigrants in Great Britain and Germany showed that the vast majority of German immigrants still identify with their home country (83%), whereas this is the case with only 19% of minorities in Britain (Koopmanns and Statham 1998).

Economic segregation has become evident in the growing income inequality between the majority and the ethnic minorities since the halt in the recruitment of foreign workers in the late 1970s. Today the unemployment rate of migrants is roughly twice that of the majority, and the foreign population is experiencing increasing impoverisation relative to the Germans. One of the reasons for these marked differences can be found in the shift in the economy and labor market from a previously productive sector to the service sector. This has re-enforced the discrimination of non-Germans, since popular opinion in Germany has it that immigrants and their offspring do not possess the necessary communicative skills required in dealing with the public. This holds true for kindergarten teachers as well as for bank employees (Beauftragte der Bundesregierung 1997).

Another reason why the situation is getting worse is the fact that the German school system systematically discriminates against children from disadvantaged family backgrounds, including those of a different ethnic origin. The OECD Programme For International Student Assessment (PISA 2000) has demonstrated that the educational system in Germany reinforces social and ethnically based difference, with privileged middle class children of German descent reaping the benefits from this system. Since education plays a pivotal role in the labor market, the situation for many migrants seems to be getting worse rather than better. In fairness, however, it has to be noted that a considerable minority within the minority – about 10% of migrant youth – perform quite well in school and are successful in academic life (Münz and Ulrich 2000). Therefore there is a growing gap within the migrant youth: on the one hand, there is the vast majority having no or very few opportunities to attain those educational and employment goals they have set for themselves, and, on the other hand, there are only a few who have the chance to succeed and realize their dreams.

Finally, there is social segregation, which can be measured, for example, by the rate of intercultural marriages or by the prevalence and intensity of friendships among school children of different ethnical background. At this point it is difficult to ascertain exactly what the situation is. All in all, there seems to be a growing acceptance of mixed marriages. This can also be said of empirical findings showing an increase in barrier-free mixing among pupils. But other findings indicate a high degree of segregation among children of different ethnical and social background in the same classroom (Münz *et al.* 1997; Dollase 1996).

The most poignant expression of social segregation, however, has to be seen in the dramatic increase in racist violence and right wing extremism in the aftermath of German unification. In the beginning of the 1990s there was an unprecedented rise in right wing extremism in both East and West Germany. The persecution of people of color and arson attacks on refugee shelters led to a public outcry in Germany. Although right wing crime declined during the late nineties, it still remains on a relatively high level (Friedrich and Förster 1997).

It is interesting to note that violent extremism is far more prevalent in East Germany than in West Germany. However, this is not true when we look at extremist attitudes. Although we find a somewhat higher degree of racist attitudes in East Germany, the main difference between East and West seems to lie in an inclination or tendency towards violent extremism. Extensive empirical research has been carried out as to the underlying causes for this racist violence. The different findings coincide in that the increase in violence can be seen as concomitant with the growing dissatisfaction of the East Germans with the democratic system (Schmidtchen 1997; Friedrich and Förster 1997; Stöss 1999; Schubarth and Stöss 2000). It is not just the high unemployment rate, as many have argued, which leads to disaffection and extremist attitudes. In fact, no correlation could be found between the rate of unemployment and extremist attitudes, i.e., political violence. But the impression that – regardless of what you do, you have no voice in the decision-making process – makes people, in particular young men, believe that they have to take things into their own hands. Violence seems to foster the illusion of controlling a situation.

Thus we can see that the modes of integration and segregation are subject not only to their specific relationship to the hegemonic Germans but also to the nature of inter-ethnic relations. Racism in East Germany, in particular in its violent form, is more prevalent than in West Germany also as a result of the rather undemocratic unification process. East Germany was expected simply to integrate into western society. Hence, the differences between the two Germanies were considered to be a *quantité négligeable* by the West Germans. The German political tradition of co-opting to authoritarian self-interest in dealing with conflicts was thus reaffirmed. This again reinforced the antidemocratic attitudes within East Germany, which in the final analysis fostered a political climate where various regions and communities of the East became "no go areas" for visible minorities.

It is interesting to note how German society responded to this development. First, a number of social support and social work programs geared towards right wing youth were established. Initially right wing extremism had been interpreted in the main as a social problem, as an expression of disorientation and social frustration of a disaffected youth without a future. However, in the meantime empirical research and ten years of social work praxis suggest that it is crucial to view this development also as a political problem and to analyze the political culture which facilitates racist attitudes and violent acts of racism. Therefore the focal point in combating right wing extremism and acts of political violence over the past few years has shifted more into the direction of establishing support groups to strengthen civil society and to promote the democratization of democracy. This means holding every individual and all institutions in society accountable for their deeds and not just projecting the problems onto a violent-prone youth. At the same time the work with these young people has been centered more on winning them over for democracy, by clearly articulating social and political responsibilities, and not merely focusing on personal and social problems. Finally, the main focus in the struggle against racism in some of the new governmental programs has shifted to offering substantial and tangible support to ethnic minorities in order to help them redress some of their grievances. This can be done in the form of taking legal action in the courts or by asking for public support on specific issues, as well as by providing the aggrieved with psychological and social counseling (Rommelspacher, Polat, and Wilpert 2002).

In conclusion, the empowerment of ethnic minorities seems to be one of the most important strategies to combat racism and promote democracy in this country, since the expression of difference is still a provocation *vis-à-vis* a political culture based on assimilation. Consistent efforts will have to be made to counteract the traditional views of social exclusion and to create the vision of a pluralist society against the powerful images of an alleged ethnic homogeneity.

Works Cited

Bade, Klaus. *Ausländer, Aussiedler, Asyl*. München: Beck, 1994.

Bar-On, Dan. *Last des Schweigens. Gespräche mit Kindern von Nazi-Tätern*. Frankfurt/Main; New York: Campus, 1993.

Beauftragte der Bundesregierung für Ausländerfragen. *Migration und Integration in Zahlen. Ein Handbuch*. Bonn, 1997.

Beger, Kai-Uwe. *Migration und Integration: eine Einführung in das Wanderungsgeschehen und die Integration der Zugewanderten in Deutschland*. Opladen: Leske und Budrich, 2000.

Davy, Ulrike. "Integration von Einwanderern: Instrumente – Entwicklungen – Perspektiven." *Die Integration von Einwanderern. Rechtliche Regelungen im europäischen Vergleich*. Ed. Ulrike Davy. Frankfurt; New York: Campus, 2001. 925–988.

Dollase, Rainer. "Die Asozialität der Gefühle. Intrapsychische Dilemmata im Umgang mit dem Fremden." Eds. Wilhelm Heitmeyer and Rainer Dollase. Frankfurt/Main: Suhrkamp, 1996. 120-141.

Friedrich, Walter, and Peter Förster. "Politische Orientierungen ostdeutscher Jugendlicher und junger Erwachsener im Transformationsprozeß." *Entwicklung und Sozialisation von Jugendlichen vor und nach der Vereinigung Deutschlands*. Eds. Hubert and Sydow. Opladen: Leske and Budrich, 1997. 17-73.

Koopmans, Ruud, and Hanspeter Kriesi. *Citizenship, National Identity and Mobilisation of the Extrem Right. A Comparison of France, Germany, the Netherlands and Switzerland*. Berlin: Wissenschaftszentrum, 1997.

Münz, Rainer. "Migration, Flucht und Vertreibung in Europa. Ein Rückblick auf das 20. Jahrhundert." *Demokratie und das Fremde Multikulturelle Gesellschaften als demokratische Herausforderung des 21. Jahrhunderts*. Ed. Erna Appelt. Innsbruck; Wien; München: Studien, 2001. 24-54.

Münz, Rainer, and E. Ralf Ulrich "Migration und zukünftige Bevölkerungsentwicklung in Deutschland." *Migrationsreport 2000 Fakten – Analysen – Perspektiven*. Eds. Klaus J. Bade and Rainer Münz. Frankfurt/Main: Campus, 2000. 23-57.

Rommelspacher, Birgit. *Schuldlos-Schuldig? Wie sich junge Frauen mit Antisemitismus auseinandersetzen*. Hamburg: Konkret Literatur, 1995.

---. *Anerkennung und Ausgrenzung. Deutschland als multikulturelle Gesellschaft.* Frankfurt/Main: Campus, 2002.

Rommelspacher, Birgit, Polat Ülger, and Czarina Wilpert. *Das CIVITAS-Programm – Eine adäquate Antwort auf Rechtsextremismus, Fremdenfeindlichkeit und Antisemitismus in den neuen Bundesländern? Die Aufbauphase.* Berlin: Alice Salomon Hochschule, 2002.

Schmidtchen, Gerhard. *Wie weit ist der Weg nach Deutschland? Sozialpsychologie der Jugend in der postsozialistischen Welt.* Opladen: Leske und Budrich, 1997.

Stöss, Richard. *Rechtsextremismus im vereinten Deutschland.* Bonn: Friedrich Ebert Stiftung, 1999.

Zuwanderung: Bericht der unabhängigen Kommission der Bundesregierung. *Zuwanderung gestalten, Integration fördern.* Berlin: Zeitbild, 2001.

Social Exclusion and Cultures of Resistance Amongst Young Male Immigrants in the "New Sweden"

Ove Sernhede

> They say on TV that immigrants have to be integrated and that we should do this and that. But how the fuck can we be integrated into society when they don't even want us there really. They shut the door, got it. That's how I see it. They shut me out of society, then they want me to participate. You understand? How can you participate when you can't even get in. /.../ I don't see myself as a member of this society, ya know. That's how I feel. I'm a Swedish citizen, I'm not going to vote. 'Cause I don't care, got it. I don't care. Why should I get mixed up in their business. It doesn't feel like my business. Even though I'm a Swedish citizen and have lived here for ten years, I don't care. Ya know, that's how I see myself. I don't want to integrate anything. I don't want to be part of…/…/…I have nothing in common with Swedish society.
> Muhammad, 20 years, Swedish citizen, born in Somalia.

The latest general election in Sweden in 2002 supported the picture of a general pattern of decreasing voter turnout. This low turnout was also one of the big issues in the post-election debates. Today, in a number of different groups within Swedish society, we see an increasingly clear tendency towards alienation and dissociation in relation to the official forms and institutions of politics. In the debates, this new pattern of development has been presented as a threat to or a crisis for democracy. Although these developments are general in nature, it is undoubtedly so that they are more prominent among young people and immigrants than among many other groups.

Muhammad, quoted above, is in many respects representative of the young people with whom I have had contact during two years through a research project on immigrant youth and their forms of culture. The most striking and common feature of the stories they have shared with me has to do with exclusion, with non-participation, with a feeling that "real Swedes don't really want to get to know us immigrants". Their stories are about experiencing that official Swedish institutions are not intended for them. Time and again, they return to the feeling of not being desirable, of not fitting in, of not having a place. Time and again, they return to the frustration of "not knowing what I should do with my life". They are Swedish, but not really. Moving to their parents' homeland is not a practicable solution either. Even though they have family and friends there, even though they enjoy visiting (if this is at all possible), and even though they may perceive themselves as more Chilean or Somalian than Swedish, the parents" homeland is still a different world than the one they grew up in and have an internalized relation to. There is no future there either. Given their feelings of non-belonging both in Sweden and their parents' homeland, many of the youth I have interviewed view the identity offered by immigrant status as their primary identity. They are not Swedish, not Chilean or Somalian, they are immigrants or, as they often call themselves, "Blackheads". These young people are brought together by the alienation of being an immigrant. All of them are "Blackheads", regardless of where they have their roots – in Europe, Latin America or Africa. "Alienation is our Nation, Reality is my Nationality" claimed one of the youngsters – with an alien passport – with connotations to the well-known rap artist Kool G Rap. The innovative cultural work these young people are involved in – and that I have taken an interest in through my research – deals with, among other things, redefining this alienation and deciding for themselves what it means. The new cultural patterns they are creating not only highlight their frustration and pain, but likewise the power and potential, the joy and community that also exists in the environments where they live their lives. Among other things, this is a matter of taking from "the Svens" their right to interpret how these environments are understood and defined. "We aren't people you should feel sorry for, I hate it when there are discussions and Swedes say "poor immigrants", we're not "poor immigrants". We have our pride you know, we're not wimps". They defend themselves against being turned into victims. This is why they have consciously taken over the epithet "Blackhead", a term originally used by xenophobic Swedes. Thus, just as blacks in the US have taken over "Nigger" and given it another meaning, young people in Angered, a suburb of Göteborg, have transformed the meaning of "blackhead".

Another common response to the situation of homelessness felt by young immigrants is to focus on their own district or suburb. This strategy is used primarily by boys and young men. In creating an identity and security, the place where you grew up, where you live, where you spend your everyday life and where you have your friends becomes a crucial factor. Among the young men I met, there is a strong need to charge with meaning and elevate the local physical environment as well as the youth community. "Hammarkullen – that's our place on earth", but this Hammarkullen is not part of Sweden, it is a "reservation", a "free zone". In relation to Sweden, Hammarkullen is another world, another country, another form of community. Thus, it is a place to which you are referred, but it is also the place you give your love because you perceive it as your home. Hammarkullen offers security and protection and is the social space for common interests.

A Tense Relation to Swedish Authorities

When, after a day's work, all the social workers, teachers, youth-club leaders and administrative staff climb into their cars and drive ten plus kilometers to the housing areas in Göteborg's inner city, they are replaced by security companies and police – "changing of the guard for the occupying power". Many I have spoken with consider the relation between Angered and the rest of Göteborg to be colonial. Given this understanding, the police have a clear mission, and in Hammarkullen in particular, young people's relationship to the police has a long and inflamed history. In the interviews, the young immigrants tell of how they have long felt provoked and harassed by the police. "If they come here with their batons and cocky attitudes then we have a cocky attitude back. Just 'cause we're some sort of underclass doesn't mean we put up with anything, ya know". Santos, a 20-year-old Peruvian, can talk at length and well about his experience of their relation to the police.

In spring 1997, when I began staying in the area, the first thing that happened was, among other things, a confrontation between youth and the police. At this time there were no neighborhood police in the area. When a 19-year-old young man was about to be seized by a police patrol, a situation arouse in which a large group of youth intervened in order to rescue their friend. The patrol car's windshield was smashed and the policemen lost control, became panicky and called in reinforcements. Within a few minutes' time, twenty-two additional police cars arrived in order to head off the "riot". The next day, big headlines were circulated in the press. Youth from Hammarkullen were depicted as an unruly mob, as hoodlums. The circumstances that, according to the young people, were the actual cause of the disturbances were not presented in the media. On television, Channel 4 was an exception. The local news desk arranged a debate between youth and the police. It became clear on this occasion that the press had not provided the whole truth. In this context, the young people did not at all appear to be hooligans, they in no way corresponded to stereotypical portrayals in the evening papers – portrayals of immigrant youth as dangerous and brutal. Instead, these young immigrants appeared to be just the opposite – articulate, mature and sober. During the live broadcast, they even invited the police to take a "class" that they intended to give, provided the police were interested. In their opinion, the police must acquire more knowledge about the life conditions of immigrant youth and the big city. Many police officers come from small towns and have no idea what it means to live in a modern, big city suburb. Their knowledge of what it means to be an immigrant is even more limited.

Adults living in the area also perceived the 22 extra patrol cars and newspaper articles to be insulting. They demanded a meeting with and explanation from the office of the chief. No one from the office came to the meeting that was called, but instead two former neighborhood police, both of whom have a good name in the district, showed up. Because neither of the officers was present during the event in question, they were naturally unable to respond to the questions posed by the indignant participants at the meeting. It was poignant to see an elderly Chilean refugee stand and take the floor. He was extremely critical of the police and said, "I have been at the soccer stadium in Santiago as political prisoner, I have seen police and the military attack people in this way, but I never thought this could happen in Olof Palme's Sweden". In order to understand how many young people view the media, we must remember that events such as this "riot" and their consequences constitute the relevant background. There is a strongly expressed aversion to all of the images of misery, poverty and trouble that the media are perceived to ration out at regular intervals. Every negative reference in the papers or on TV is an insult. The media are not thought of as independent or neutral and critical institutions. On the contrary, the perception is that the function of the media – especially the evening press – is to paint immigrants in black colors, thereby identifying them as second-class citizens before "the Swedes".

Victor, a 19-year-old of Latin American origin, comments on the media-made image of his own suburb:

> Hammarkullen is really a reservation. Rinkeby is too, in Stockholm. When I'm in Hammarkullen everything feels okay. Everybody badmouths Hammarkullen, but nobody's been there. That's why people don't want to be anywhere else, 'cause then things aren't okay. Now I'm in Hammarkullen, it's another world. I know everybody and everybody's just like me. When I leave Hammarkullen I come to Sweden, and when I'm in Sweden I feel discriminated against. It doesn't feel like Sweden is my country and it never will. Even if… I have a theory that the world is where you want to live. If a place feels good, you should live there. But Sweden doesn't feel like my country. When I look around I only see white, blond people. I really don't want to be part of that society. There's no reason to 'cause I don't feel at home there anyway. Then maybe you wonder "why the hell are you here then". There really are a lot of problems. I was born here, ya know, and I don't know what I'm going to do with my life really. There just shouldn't be any barriers.

New Patterns of Poverty in Europe

Since the middle of the 1980s, an intense debate has raged among sociologists and other social scientists about patterns of marginalization and poverty on the European continent as well as in the United Kingdom. The development towards a "post-industrial" society has implied a growing social polarization in many countries. The rise of new forms of social exclusion has pushed an increasing number of groups into marginalization and ultimately into exclusion. The forms and intensities involved in this process of mounting class differentiation are indeed varying. However, it is still possible to discern certain common tendencies in the emerging new Europe.

In order to explain this development, politicians refer regularly and compulsively to the "economic crisis". Simultaneously, it is a fact that GNP and the accumulated wealth witnessed a strong growth in the entire European Union during the past two, three decades. Luxury and poverty have always existed side by side. However, the present situation offers something new in the form of growing gaps between the world of affluence and that of scarcity. Neither millionaires nor the destitute have at any time during the post-war period been so numerous as now. According to official statistics, there are 52 million poor people, 17 million unemployed and three million homeless in the EU. These figures are rising every day, while an improved competitive position has moved the European economy into a phase of strong expansion.

A background element of importance in this development is the new international division of labor. In addition, there are crucial structural changes in the economy which have created a situation where, for example, the new IT sector is putting greater demands on labor. Economies require highly qualified people with a dramatically increased competence, while a number of tasks in traditional industries are eliminated. The simple equation is that there are no jobs for a growing army of "redundancies". The effect on immigrants and refugees who have moved to the suburbs of European cities in recent years is that they, too, are facing growing difficulties in entering the labor market. The permanency of contemporary patterns of poverty are clearly linked to processes of de-industrialization and globalization. The French sociologist Pierre Bourdieu characterizes the new patterns of poverty that grow out of these structural changes as the "modern misery", and this new situation has emerged independent of the state of the economies. Those who carry the new destitution on their shoulders have easily been disarmed by their marginal positions and their heterogeneity. The political machines of established interests find it menacing to be in any sense identified with or much less a mouthpiece for this "modern misery".

Immigrationhood, Alienationhood

The dismantling of the institutions of the welfare state is at the root of contemporary poverty. The British sociologist Scott Lash has called it an "institutional deficit", which is particularly evident in urban, ghetto-like environments where modern misery is more manifest. The American scholar William Julius Wilson has stressed the pattern of synchronization between developments in Europe and the United States. The French sociologist Loic Wacquant has, on the other hand, found decisive differences. One important such difference is constituted by the heterogeneous ghettos in Europe. Another difference is that, in Europe, the demarcation line between the socially excluded and the rest of society is not as clearly related to the categories race or ethnicity as it is in the US. There has been a great debate on how to characterize this new situation. Scholars on the right argue that the development of the welfare state produced a social strata they call "the new underclass", a strata unwilling to work and deeply dependent on welfare subsidies. The opposite view of this new situation does not blame the victims but the structural changes in the European economy during the last two, three decades.

Those marginalized groups of mobile immigrants or refugees who are labeled the "new poor" or the "outcasts" on the Continent have, during the past ten to fifteen year period, been forming ghettos everywhere in Europe – Moss Side (Manchester), Niewe Westen (Rotterdam), Val d'Argent (Paris), Rinkeby (Stockholm), Angered (Göteborg) and Rosengård (Malmö). All of these areas are involved in what Wacquant defines as a territorial stigmatization process. The societal and medial discourse is demonizing the conditions of life in these areas such that, both inside and outside of them, fear and insecurity are being created. A moral panic is instigated by stereotypes about criminality, race, culture and religious antagonisms, which additionally exacerbates conditions for people who are already side tracked by poverty and alienation. The social tensions are growing, and Lash, instead of asking "if", is asking "when" the European version of the Rodney King affair will occur – and where: in Berlin, Marseilles or Rotterdam?

The situation in metropolitan areas in Sweden - Stockholm, Göteborg and Malmö - is that 40% of all children and young people between zero to seventeen years of age live in "exposed urban districts", to cite a parliamentary committee on Big City Conditions. The majority of people in these districts have foreign backgrounds. The largest proportions of youngsters with immigrant origins are to be found in districts with extremely low incomes. In 1994, the disposable income among families with children in Rosengård (Malmö) was 156.000 SEK (13.000 British pounds) lower *per annum* than the average income in the city of Stockholm. In Göteborg and Malmö, there are districts with extremely low incomes that coincide with a 90% immigrant population and where more than 50% of the children between zero to six years of age have unemployed parents. These circumstances have put Sweden into a state of shock. The so-called "Swedish model", the famous welfare state, is eroding. The situation cannot, of course, be compared to conditions in the United States, where one in two black children lives in poverty. Nevertheless, the idea of the Swedish welfare state is crushed. Sweden has for some time also been entering the "two-thirds society". The full employment of 1990 became, in real terms, 15-20% unemployment overnight In Göteborg, a classic working-class city with half a million inhabitants of whom nearly 150.000 have an immigrant background, social entitlements increased by 100% between 1990 and 1993.

Research on the new areas of poverty in the European metropolitan districts suggests that, in contrast to the traditional working-class quarters where poverty was an integrated part of the culture, the new areas are suffering from a lack of solidarity and community spirit. The local, collective and territorial identity, which previously provided security and a feeling of self-assertiveness, is now replaced by instability in the very same districts. There exists, it is claimed, an uncertainty and an alienation in relation to the rest of society. At the same time, the internal conditions are inculcated by competition and conflict-ridden antagonisms between different groups. These patterns may, of course, also be discerned in Sweden. The new immigrant-dominated suburban districts in the three Swedish metropolitan areas constitute fragile communities, the mark of which is extreme ethnic heterogeneity. For many adults who see their living in a particular district as a temporary solution, the social room provided by this district is a rather weak basis for any community spirit. Instead, it is the family and the commonality of one's own ethnic group that are charged with a new meaning.

The Hammer Hill Click

Things are different for the young. At day-care, everyone plays with everyone else, and in school, you co-operate with others who have different ethnic backgrounds. During leisure time, you are out in the streets and cultivate friendships that supersede the ethnic boundaries drawn by the parental culture. All adolescents are in the process of seeking both their outer and inner selves; that is part of their identity work. In these multi-ethnic areas, the constant encounters with young people from other cultures, with Swedish society and with today's a multi-facetted, global and medialized youth-culture, imply that new points of departure are created for identification processes, which by necessity are embedded in adolescent identity work.

Among the contact groups I observed during the year I studied immigrant youth in Hammarkullen (Angered), one of the more salient features is their openness to absorbing and testing the different expressions, articulations and outlooks on the world inherent in different cultures. Although most of the youngsters I met are Swedish citizens, they do not consider themselves as Swedes. On the other hand, adopting their parents' national identity is not self-evident either. "Cassius" from Tunisia tells me:

> I'm not Swedish, I never could be Swedish 'cause this society don't want me, but I'm not Tunisian either, but of course I'm more Tunisian than Swede. You see ... I couldn't go back to Tunisia 'cause I have no future there. I've been going to school here in Hammarkullen, I have all my friends here, I have my life here – but this is not Sweden – it's Hammarkullen and Hammarkullen is a reservation, there are no Swedes living here so it's not Sweden – it's Hammarkullen. It's like the Third World in the middle of the first world, if you see what I mean. I don't give a shit about nationality, I belong to the Hip Hop Nation. That means I have more in common
> with Hip hop people in Berlin, Cape Town and Mexico City than I have with someone that don't think like me, someone that's from the other side of this town. We out here are all one, even though we come from everywhere – you know we are citizens of the world – what keeps us together is that we are all on the outside, we don't have no place in society

In Hammarkullen, a local version of Hip hop culture is quiet strong. I have spent most of my time with a group of ten to fifteen young men, aged seventeen to twenty-five, who make rap-music. They are apart of a bigger Hip hop collective of fifty young people who preferably make rap-music, produce graffiti and break dance. The members of this rap-group have their origins in Africa, Latin America and the Middle East. They regard themselves as constituting an ethnic alliance, the task of which is to represent not only the young from Hammer Hill (to which they have literally re-baptized their district), but to speak for all immigrant youth from all suburbs in Sweden. This collective aptly calls itself "The Hammer Hill Click", and it is working very hard at creating respect and goodwill for their own suburb. Their loyalty to the area (district) is steadfast. A territorial mythology is cultivated that constitutes a kind of "nationalism of the neighborhood", which is strongly reminiscent of the way working-class lads once upon a time launched their strategies in order to symbolically charge the quarters of their own upbringing.

Being a "click" implies that what they do is more than music, it is politics as well as music; break-dance and graffiti. They have no problem combining the cultural with the political, the aesthetical with the ethical. Being a "click" means that they, in spite of their different origins and creeds, are an inseparable unit. Within this Click, every individual has a fundamental right to claim his or her religious or ethnic particularity and to represent any branch of rap-music, as long as he or she is loyal to the defined common task of the group. The task is to regard yourself as a soldier with music as a weapon or to be, as the Click says, a "microphone prophet". The group's lyrics deal with police brutality, discrimination and racism in Swedish society; and they embrace friendship and gang solidarity, reverence to Allah and Islam, the history of Latin America, everyday life in the suburb, and so on. During spring of 1998, the group issued a mini-CD. One song is entitled "88-soldiers". When I asked what they mean by that title, one of the Latin Americans in the group responded: "Man, you must think, think for yourself, what do you think Man".

After some intense thinking work, dismissing the explanation that they are a total of 88 persons, I realized that it has to do with the symbolism in figures that the Neo-nazis employ when they render cryptic greetings to Hitler. H is the eighth letter in the alphabet, and 88 is consequently HH or Heil Hitler. Thus I asked if it is just something the Nazis use to praise Hitler? The whole gang burst into laughter and one of them said:

> Man, you are a wimp, sure - we rip those symbols off the Nazis and create total confusion for them, you dig Man. In one year's time they can't go around in the city any more with their 88-tattoos 'cause we've snatched their symbols. For us 88 means Hammer Hill (the literal translation of the name of the suburb Hammarkullen) and 88-soldiers represents our being soldiers, the soldiers of Hammarkullen and we've ready for war. We've had enough, we don't want to take all this crap any more, do you get it Man, you get it. In this song everybody is there, all 12 have their own rhymes about their own thing. Muhammad and B-boy speak for the blacks, for their people and their religion...you hear that they rap around Allah and "breaking the law" and... then we Latinos are coming with the message to our people about the brown ones, you understand Man... then we are creating certain rhymes together so it becomes "niggaz and latinos got to unite n' fight" and that sort of thing, you get it Man. You know, the song begins with different sounds like that, then it eases its way over to violins, beautiful and disturbing like that, then there are sounds showing that there is a war going on, you understand and then we come in and talk cool, first saying that we aren't gonna take any more crap and then...we really get going...

The title of another song is "El Mensaje" (The Message); it was written by two of the Latinos in the group. The lyrics tell about the Mapoto tribe, the only Latin American Indians that the Spanish conquistadors never defeated. The song is about the fate of the Indians, it tells us that their history is just about the same as that of the blacks from Africa. Their histories are parallel: the plundering and the enslavement by the white man, by Europe. This is the situation still: all exploited people must unite against "the white man's love for money", and then the Mapotos is a tribe to identify with - "no retreat, no surrender". The song starts with an aggressive Spanish guitar, which symbolizes the scent of gold and the hubris of the conquistadores. Gradually, this chord recedes into an Indian melody-line that becomes stronger and clearer. This folklore-inspired melody is played on an old Indian string instrument and symbolizes the resistance on the part of the Indians. The song is in praise to those Indian tribes who were driven back farther and farther up in the Andes and whom the Spaniards never managed to subdue. Even if these boys do not have any Indian ancestry, they strongly identify with these South American Indians. When I asked if any one of them had Indian blood, they told me that it does not matter. It is not a question of blood in that sense, the identification is grounded on another, symbolic level.

> Even though I'm not an Indian, what the Spaniards did hurts me. It's too bad the culture will disappear, for other people too. We don't want to lose it. Even if I don't have Indian blood, we're proud to come from a country where there were Indians, and in the song – The Message – we're trying to say that all Latin Americans are the same people and that we all have the same blood. A long time ago we experienced the same thing and we have the same fate. We can gain power if we just unite, but it's not that way today, we're not united, in Sweden we're different – Chileans, Bolivians and all. But we feel like one and the same people, like Latinos. Europe has tried to screw us. We shouldn't be against each other – it should be us against them... and them – that you can think of however you like, ya know...

On the CD, there are two more songs "One is more commercial you know like more funky gangsta-shit and it is called "West Coast Slang", whereas the name of the other one is "Pig hunting season" which deals with police hostility towards us and how we are against the police".

The most palpable feature of my contact with this multi-ethnic Hip hop collective remains their definition of themselves as representatives of and spokesmen for what they themselves call a "new underclass". In one sense they are unusual. There are few other politically articulate groups of young immigrants who see themselves as "soldiers" and the multi-ethnic cultural expression they create as armory. In another sense they are quite common. In several comparable districts around Sweden, similar meetings and fusions are taking place. Each area has its specific preconditions, such as its own specific history, its own ethnic composition etc., thus resulting in different youth cultures being created in different areas. Although local variation is great, there are still certain fundamental patterns that characterize most of the immigrant-dominated suburbs irrespective of their location – Stockholm, Göteborg or Malmö. One is the subordinated role of girls in street cultures that outwardly give shape to the patterns of development outlined above. Another striking feature concerns the identification with and impact of those lifestyles and ideals formed in the frustrations and wrath of the North American ghetto culture.

Black Culture, White Youth

From cultural studies we know that, since the inter-war period, certain youth subcultures, both in the United States and in Europe, have been inspired by, and even taken over, elements of African American culture. From the emergence of the first modern US youth cultures of the 1920s, when black hot-jazz was at the center of interest, over to bebop, rhythm-and-blues, soul, funk and reggae, and up to the rap music of today, Afro American music has constituted a central element in youth cultures. Today, Hip hop or the culture within which rap-music has grown appears increasingly to be the obvious underclass culture of global urbanity. This is also true of patterns in Sweden. Young men of today not only listen to "black music"; they also walk, talk and dress like Afro Americans more than ever before. Some have acquired the label "White Niggers" or "Wiggers" whereas others call themselves "Black Albinos". For instance, by claiming that "blackness is a state of mind" and not of the skin, the more reflexive and articulate parts of this youth culture deconstruct given perceptions and reach through proclamatory statements and song texts into that academic discussion that has long maintained that race and ethnicity are political and cultural constructions.

During previous decades, the middle class often dominated the movement of jazz freaks and blues or soul fanatics, who rendered black culture an exotic flavor – a flavor that came in handy when defying and challenging the parental culture. The remnants of this pattern still exists, of course, but what is new is that it is no longer middle class youth who dominate in terms of interest in the Afro American culture. This is rather the mission of the new immigrant youth, who certainly also cultivate romantic ideas of the ghetto culture. The decisive element causing immigrant youngsters to identify with this particular culture is the analogy between their own situation and that of the black population in the USA. Their fascination with the Afro-American culture is founded on its aesthetic expressions, which serve as a point of departure for the formulation of their own experiences of alienation and discrimination, while cultural codes cry out for resistance and offer alternatives to the established identity and life patterns of Swedish society.

Many of these young people perceive the traditional Swedish institutions, parties and ideologies as non-credible and not created for them. "You know I actually know a lot about politics, but I may never be recognized for that. You only have to look at the Swedish parliament to see how many blackheads you find there...you know the normal and ordinary sort of politics is not for us", declared Santos, a Latin American 20-year-old. Santos speaks with some authority, since he has lived in Sweden since the age of 3. For him, like for many of his friends, the ghetto culture (black as well as Hispanic) seems also to be the only adequate expression for political resistance. The poses, jargon and attitudes of this culture do offer – in a menacing way – a counter-identity that invokes respect.

Identification with African American culture does, however, contain a dualism. On the one hand, it appears as if the openness of this culture, its "call-and-response" structure, leads to embryos of new communities and cultural models. Its aesthetic codes, particularly evident in the music, constitute a language that in certain respects loosens up ethnic boundaries or builds bridges across them. Such processes may create new forms of alliances and amalgamations. Herein we find a potential that may function as a basis for constructive dialogues and learning processes between those youngsters who employ these cultural patterns and Swedish society.

On the other hand, we can also see today how marginalization and powerlessness contribute to creating a fascination with the criminal gang culture of the ghettos, which in real terms may reinforce alienation, exclusion and segregation. Those tendencies of hostility towards the dominating culture – tendencies that already exist in certain circles where many immigrant youngsters grow up – may be reinforced through identification with the most uncompromising and violence-centered aspects of the ghetto culture. It may, thus, cement and legitimate irrepressible, confrontational stances that are festering in certain environments. This is a likely scenario if the growing tendencies towards segregation and marginalization cannot be broken. Increasing numbers of immigrant youth will face mounting difficulties in entering Swedish social life. Many already find themselves at an impasse and see no other way but to turn against society. Far from everyone has the constructive and articulated political ambition of The Hammer Hill Click, who, via their rap-music, are knocking on the door to be let into Swedish society.

Rap – Abundant Branches of Styles
What is rap, and what does the ghetto culture look like? Rap emerged in the US east coast black ghettos during the latter half of the 1970s. It was then rooted in the oral and musical traditions of black culture, while also sensitive to the landscape of sounds in modern society as a whole. With simple means, a music of the streets was created, which in a new and effective way publicly expressed the brutal reality of many blacks. Young blacks communicated with their own people through rap.

Today, rap has a rich content, and the performers are not exclusively black. But it was in fact the hard-core black nationalist inspired rap that got the attention of non-blacks. This politically engaged rap began to flourish during the second half of the 1980s, mainly through the "black consciousness rap" performed by Public Enemy, a group parroting the black Panthers. This rap was inculcated with social realism and criticism. Soon it had a foothold on the American west coast, and Los Angeles became the center of its further unfolding. This development was against the background of the ghetto gang cultures, police brutality, internal wars and dope pushing the most salient themes. Militant exhibitionists such as Public Enemy were overrun by a street culture, "gangsta", which not only gave expression to criticism of injustice in a racist society, but which also articulated weapon fetishism, contempt for women and romaticizing of violence. In this context, the so-called gangster-rap arose. For some time now, this form of rap-music has been well established in Sweden, particularly in the metropolitan suburbs.

The currents of migration, processes of marginalization and patterns of segregation that profoundly transformed Sweden during the 1990s, tend to make immigration almost synonymous with social exclusion. Comparing the Swedish situation with developments in France, the French sociologist Etienne Balibar denotes these conditions as "racism without race". As we know from youth culture research, cultures developed by the young often make visible antagonisms and conflicts that exist below the surface of society. The immigrant young men I interviewed in "Los Angered", Göteborg, do not expect anything from Swedish society. They are forced to grow up in a society in which ethnic boundaries are inflicted and where social inequality is transformed into cultural differences. The social and cultural logic at work here leads to a situation in which young people's sub-cultural resistance also adopts ethnified forms of appearance. The ghetto culture's poses, jargon and attitudes tend to offer an exclusive counter-identity – for "blackheads" only. The young Swedes who have been demoted to second-class citizens by the "two-thirds society", who are just as excluded as immigrant youth, find their identity and forms of resistance in cultural expressions with other ethnic overtones and political preferences. The most desperate struggle for recognition, belonging and respect is found among these two groups of young people.

In the cultures developed by youth, antagonisms and conflicts that exist under the surface are made visible. Thus, the youth culture can be likened to a seismograph. The young immigrants living in big city suburbs are in many ways – in spite of the fact that they create expressive cultures – invisible. Segregation has deported them to demarcated reservations where contact with the surrounding society is extremely limited. In this context, music and other cultural forms of expression are important. Culture gives an individual the opportunity to give form to and work through his or her situation, not least because it creates the conditions for self-understanding and makes possible the development of collective action strategies. Culture is also a channel through which a person's situation can be communicated to others – a channel that makes the terms of one person's life visible to the rest of society. An important part of the work of breaking the patterns of segregation deals with offering young people in these areas - immigrants as well as Swedes, young men as well as young women – the opportunity to present themselves, thereby creating arenas where they can stand out and be seen. This is especially important for work aimed at anchoring more deeply the processes of democracy. The growth of new forms of youth culture in multi-ethnic suburbs carries with it a criticism of the most recent decades' societal development – a criticism we can no longer overlook. However, in the public political discussion, there is a tendency to deny or shut one's eyes to this development. This attitude originates in a non-articulated, but nonetheless highly present hope that the last few decades were merely incidental. There is, without a doubt, a desire (though not always articulated) that the old order will be re-established, that the old Swedish "people's home" will be re-created. But history is an irreversible process. This is the New Sweden, and we must do more than simply learn to treat the new reality as the differences and diversification this new society has created. We must also be open to the new opportunities entailed in this new situation.

Works Cited

Ålund, Aleksandra. "Wrestling with Ghost. Transcultural Bricolage and New Communities." *Paradoxes of Multiculturalism*. Eds. Aleksandra Åhlund and Carl-Ulrik Schierup. Aldershot: Avebury, 1991. 9-36.

Back, Les. *New Ethnicity and Urban Culture*. London: UCL, 1996.

Berman, Marshall. "Close to the Edge. Reflections on Rap." *Tikkun* 8, 2 (1993):

Cohen, Phil. "'It's Racism What Dunnit': Hidden Narratives in Theories of Racism." *Race, Culture & Difference*. Eds. James Donald and Ali Rattansi. London: Sage, 1992. 62-103.

---. "Labouring under Whiteness." *Displacing Whiteness*. Ed. R. Frankenberg. New York: Duke UP, 1997.

Ehn, Billy. "Youth and Multiculturalism." *Ethnicity in Youth Culture*. Eds. Cecilia Palmgren, Karin Lövgren and Göran Bolin. Stockholm: USU/JMK, 1992. 47-65.

Gilroy, Paul. *There Ain't No Black In The Union Jack*. London: Unwin Hyman, 1987.

---. *The Black Atlantic. Modernity and Double Consciousness*. London: Verso, 1993.

Jones, Simon. *Black Culture, White Youth*. London: MacMillan, 1988.

Lash, Scott. "The Making of an Underclass: Neoliberalism versus Corporatism." *Economic Restructuring and Social Exclusion*. Eds. Philip Brown and Rosemary Crompton. London: UCL, 1994. 178-211.

Røgilds, Flemming. *Stemmer i et grænseland*. Köpenhamn: Politisk Revy, 1995.

Sernhede, Ove. "Youth and Black Culture as "Otherness"." *MIGRATION* nr 3/4. 261-293.

---. "Black Music, White Adolescence. Oidipal Rivalery, Absent Fathers and Masculinity." *Negotiating Identities*. Raoul Granqvist and Aleksandra Åhlund. Amsterdam: Rodopi, 1995. 166-210.

---. "White Youth, Black Culture." *Facing Modern Youth and Subcultures*. Ed. Peter Mikkelsen. Copenhagen: ETEN – Report from European Teacher Education Network, 1996. 49-64.

---. "Waiting for Mandela." *Soundings* 8 (1998). 163-176.

---. "Exoticism and Death as a Modern Taboo." *Without Guarantees. In Honour of Stuart Hall*. Eds. Paul Gilroy, Lawrence Grossberg and Angela McRobbie. London: Routledge, 1999. 302-319.

Wacquant, Loic J.D. "Urban Outcasts: Stigma and Division in the Black American Ghetto and the French Urban Periphery." *International Journal of Urban and Regional Research*, 17:3 (1993).

Wilson, Williams Julius. *The Ghetto Underclass. Social Science Perspectives*. Newbury Park: Sage, 1993.

When Tradition Becomes Fashionable:
The Case of Young Turkish Women in Belgium

Christiane Timmerman

Migrants, by definition, have left behind their familiar surroundings and must acquaint themselves with a new environment. Establishing a comfortable socio-cultural niche in a new society is not an easy task, though. When people feel insecure because of a lack of structure in their lives, they will inevitably search for something to hold on to and, consequently, might withdraw into a space where they feel safe and confident. In a confrontation with a bewildering "modern" society, so-called "tradition" may represent a haven of security where self-esteem can be regained. As such, "new" lifestyles, mores, attitudes and ideologies that are in some way related to or show affinity with so-called "tradition" are more likely to be accepted. The success of Islamism can be explained in these terms. In this paper, I consider certain aspects of this dynamic among young Turkish women in Belgium.

As in other West-European countries, the first wave of Turkish immigrants arrived in Belgium in the 1960s, as a result of bilateral agreements between the two countries (Atalik and Beeley 1992). Although a halt to immigration was called in 1974, the Turkish population in Belgium continued to grow steadily. In 1993, some 88.269 people with Turkish nationality were registered in Belgium, which represented 0,9 percent of the country's total population (Poulain 1994). In 1999 this figure dropped to 70.701 Turkish nationals. However, we have to keep in mind that a substantial part of the Turkish population adopted Belgian nationality. For example, from 1994 till 1998, 48.230 foreigners adopted the Belgian nationality, among them a high proportion of Turkish nationals. The majority of the Turkish immigrants came from rural areas in Central Anatolia, especially from the region around Emirdag, a small town in the Province of Afyon. The region is arid, poor, and strongly affected by emigration. By Belgian standards, most Turkish immigrants belong to the lower socio-economic strata (Manço and Manço 1992; Kesteloot, De Decker and Manço 1997).

In this article, I rely on my doctoral research (from 1989 to 1996), which focused on the relation between education, socio-cultural praxis and ethnicity[1] among young women subscribing to three different perspectives in Turkish society (Timmerman 1999). These perspectives were expressed in terms of the social and spatial origin of the

When Tradition Becomes Fashionable: The Case of Young Turkish Women in Belgium

women. The groups consisted of young women from the immigrant Turkish community in Belgium, from a rural emigration area in Turkey (namely Emirdag), and from a metropolitan middle class milieu in Istanbul. For the present purpose, I shall focus on the group of Turkish immigrant girls in Belgium. Also a study we conducted on the social networks of Turkish women of the second generation[2] and a research on the marriages between Turkish newcomers and settled immigrants in Flanders[3] provided us with relevant information.

Methodology

During my fieldwork in Belgium (1989-1996), I was involved with several socio-cultural organizations for immigrants. Young Turkish immigrant women themselves had established one of these. The women in charge of this organization had succeeded in finding their way in Belgian society; the girls with whom they worked, however, were still in that process. I taught a Dutch language course there for several years, and was also involved in several other activities. Another socio-cultural organization in which I was active was run by Belgian social workers. I worked with this organization for five years, participating in activities organized for second-generation immigrant girls.[4] More specifically I was active in the "girls association" of the organization. I was also employed as a psychologist at a health center consulted mainly by Turkish immigrants. A psychological consultation is the medium par excellence to gain insight into personal experiences. Although this setting provided me with very valuable background information, I did not "recruit" participants from it for my research.

About one hundred Turkish immigrant girls participated in the field research. They had all arrived in Belgium before the age of twelve. With the exception of four girls, they all came from families hailing from the Turkish countryside. Their parents had received very little education. Just eight percent of the mothers and 25 percent of the fathers were fluent in one of Belgium's national languages (Dutch, French or German). It was clear from our information that our sample was representative of the socio-economic situation of Turkish immigrants in Belgium.

In the two other studies we conducted in-depth interviews respectively with 46 Turkish women of the second generation and with forty Turkish newcomers.

Backed by a Nationalistic Heritage

POeople who are trying to find their way in a new society must inevitably deal with many uncertainties. They are confronted with different lifestyles, different mores and values and a different social environment. Quite predictably in such circumstances, they will tend to question their own identity. In such confusing situations, people will often seek what they perceive as their "authentic" identity, defined by so-called "tradition" and "culture", and legitimated by descent (Akbar 1995: 26-45). They will, in other words, seek an ethnic identity that, according to Frederik Barth (1969: 13), classifies a person in terms of his basic, most general identity, presumptively determined by his origin and background.

The existence of vivid nationalism in Turkey itself is conducive to the cultivation of a Turkish ethno-national identity among Turks living abroad. "Turkish Republican Nationalism" or Kemalism became the national ideology of the Turkish Republic.[5] Kemalism strove to turn Turkey into a modern nation, united around a single Turkish culture (Ross 1981). In order to change the religious-dynastic state of the Ottoman Empire into a modern capitalistic state, secularism inevitably had to become one of the cornerstones of the new society (Kandiyoti 1991: 22-47). The Kemalist perception of secularism meant not so much separation of state and religion as control of the state over religion (Zürcher 1993: 195). The caliphate was abolished in 1924. In that same year, the Sharia code was abandoned. Two years later, a new civil code, based on that of Switzerland, and a new penal code, based on that of Italy, were introduced (Tapper 1991). Though Islam was to be excluded from public life, it was nonetheless allowed to keep its significance within the private sphere (Meeker 1994: 31-63). While a folk Islamic value system still dominated private life, a Kemalist inspired worldview determined social life: "(I)n most provincial villages and towns (...) individuals learned this Islamic language of interpersonal relationships at an early age from relatives, friends and neighbors. Only later did they learn nationalist ideology, in the more formal and less nurturing context of secondary school or military service" (Meeker 1994: 33).

Meanwhile, a new form of Islam arose in the Middle East. The centralization of the newly established states and their participation in the world economy altered the structure of Middle Eastern society profoundly. In the new urban context, "folk" Islam lost much of its significance (Lindholm 1998). As Gellner (1994: 19) asserts, Islam had quite a different meaning for the rural population than it had for the bourgeoisie: "If the prosperous bourgeoisie looked to scripturalism for a confirmation of its comfortable life-style, the lower orders looked to more ecstatic religion for an escape from their own miserable condition". The newly urbanized masses tried to adapt to city life by practising a "rule-oriented" rather than a "saint-invoking" style of religion. Orthodox Islam, which used to be a privilege of the cultural elite at the center of society, now came to dominate society as a whole. "High Islam" is geared to an anonymous, mobile society (Gellner 1994: 24). It is this form of Islam that has been recruited by Islamism.

Although the basic principles of Islam are incompatible with ethno-nationalism, Islamism may be regarded as an alternative nationalist ideology that has little in common with traditional popular Islam (Eickelman and Piscatori 1996: 100). Much like secular nationalism, Islamism has succeeded in providing a new self-image for people who are no longer able to identify with a position in their native village, lineage, clan or tribe. To many Muslims, Islamism fulfills the role of an "authentic" nationalism that is, moreover, suitable to the demands of modern society (Gellner 1994: 23). Islamism seeks to offer a social alternative to the models of development that were imposed by the dominating neo-colonial presence of the superpowers (Sivan 1992: 96-108). This has contributed to "the appeal that Islam holds as a source of dignity and autonomy in the face of what are perceived to be successive defeats at the hands of an omnipresent, controlling West" (Bilgrami 1992: 832). Hostility towards the West is a common element of Islamism (Toprak 1993).

The phenomenon of Islamism has spread through the Islamic world since the establishment in Cairo of the Muslim Brothers by Hasan al-Banna (1928) (Badran 1991: 209; Juergersmeyer 1993: 58). For several decades, Islamist discourse was the only available medium in the Middle East for ventilating dissident opinions (Juergersmeyer, 1993: 59). According to Kandiyoti (1991: 8), Islamism can be seen as the instrument of the common people to indicate their alienation from the Westernized elite. Large groups of the population felt frustrated and thought that social justice was not being adequately served by the present system. In this context the message of social justice brought by the Islamists was very appealing. People were impressed by the activism of the Muslim Brothers, who were able to meet their needs more effectively (Ahmed 1992: 193).

Onis (1997: 345-347) explains the success of Islamism, at the expense of secular nationalism, in the context of an intensive process of globalization in the economic and cultural domain. This global tendency gives rise to a paradox: as a result of greater socio-economic uncertainty, people expect more from the nation-state, while, on the other hand, the nation-state loses its capacity for meeting these demands. By consequence, the secular nation-state relinquishes authority, and Islamism is able to fill the vacuum thus created. Islamism wants to improve the quality of urban society. It can count on strong support from young people belonging to the new middle classes, more specifically the lower middle classes with a rural background. Ahmed (1992: 222) describes these young people as follows: "(...) they are educationally and professionally upwardly mobile (...) and are confronting a bewildering, anonymous, cosmopolitan city life for the first time, a city life in which vivid inequalities, consumerism and materialism, foreign mores, and unscrupulous business practices linked to foreign presence, whether Western or Arab, are glaringly apparent." As a result of their traditional socialization, the values of Islamism are more familiar to them than those of the city. Affiliation with Islamism gives something to hold on to in a disorienting world; it holds out the prospect of belonging "again" to a community (Ahmed 1992: 223).

The new ideology also caught on in Turkey. Since the early 1990s, political Islam has been the most potent "threat" to the country's secular society. The shaky balance between a folk Islamic value system determining private life and a Kemalist system dominating the public domain has been profoundly disturbed in the last decades by the rise of Islamism. Contrary to a folk Islamic frame of reference, Islamism aims to control all aspects of society, both private and public (Roy 1992).

It is clear then that nationalism, both secular and religious, is well established in Turkey. As the links between Turkish emigrants living abroad and the Turkish motherland remain very close, this nationalism influences these migrants' conception of their lives in the new country.

Creating Distinction by Tradition

Atatürk's slogan "*ne mutlu Türküm diyene*" (what happiness for the person who can say "I am a Turk") is also a significant reality for most Turkish immigrants in Belgium, irrespective of their ideological orientation. Although nearly all of the ethnic Turkish girls who participated in this study were born in Belgium and are likely to spend the rest of their lives here, they all defined themselves firmly as "Turks". Turkish nationalism, then, is a significant element in the context of migration. A collective name can be an emblem of belonging to an ethnic community. Through a name – Turk – one distinguishes oneself from the others and summarizes the essence of one's identity.

However, the pattern of socio-cultural praxis among young Turkish immigrant women varies considerably. A considerable proportion participates fully in Western society. Their presence in public life remains quasi unnoticed. On the other hand, the group that wishes to distinguish itself from the "others" in Belgian society is becoming increasingly prominent. Some even try to cultivate these perceived differences. In establishing a clear and well-defined socio-cultural niche of their "own", so-called "tradition" and "culture" play a crucial role.

Turkish immigrants regard Islam as part of their cultural heritage. Moreover, it is noticeable that Islamic consciousness is growing within the Turkish community in Belgium. This Islamic awareness is engendered - as explained above – by the popularity of Islamism in Turkey specifically and in the Middle East in general. Furthermore, the way in which such a nationalistic heritage is interpreted is strongly influenced by the concrete reality of the context of immigration. In other words, certain inherent characteristics of Islamism itself and the condition of being a Turkish immigrant in Belgium contribute to the success of Islamism within the Turkish community in this country.

Twenty years ago it was unusual in Belgium to see young Turkish girls wearing a headscarf. Today, young women in "Islamic dress" are a very visible group within the Turkish immigrant community. Turks who return to the immigrant community in Belgium after spending previous years in Turkey tend to feel that Islam has become more "militant" during their absence. They notice that Islam has, generally speaking, become more popular in the Turkish immigrant community.

Milli Görüs[6], the ideological movement of the pro-Islamic but closed down *Refah Partisi* (Welfare Party) and *Fazilet Partisi* (Virtue Party) and their heirs the *Saadet Partisi* (Party of Happiness) and the *Adet ve Kalkinma Partisi* (the Party for Justice and Development) in Turkey, is most representative of Islamism in Belgium. *Milli Görüs* has become well established in Europe, with headquarters in Cologne. *Milli Görüs* aims at the economic and social integration of the Turkish immigrant community as a whole (Manço 1992: 265). Besides religious activities, *Milli Görüs* provides a whole range of educational and socio-cultural activities for its members. Many of these initiatives are targeted specifically at youngsters. It organizes sports and recreational activities, as well as language courses. As they possess a solid infrastructure, besides well-equipped sports accommodation and comfortable meeting places, they have a broad appeal. *Milli Görüs* also offers material support to its members in the form of scholarships and loans.

Several girls who participated in the research had started attending meetings of the local *Milli Görüs*. As a result, they had begun to pay more attention to the formalistic signifiers they attributed to Islam. For example, *Milli Görüs* seems to pay considerable attention to a proper Islamic diet. It is common knowledge that pork and alcohol are forbidden. However, it is far less self-evident that ready-made food may contain "unclean" ingredients. Therefore, *Milli Görüs* has drawn up lists of all forbidden ingredients, so that believers could check every packet of food before consuming it. The girls attending the meetings of the association also deemed it important that they should abide by the "rules of Islam" in relation to food as prescribed by *Milli Görüs*. Organizations such as *Milli Görüs* thus put a great deal of emphasis on formal aspects that highlight their being different from "the others". Food, dress code and even the decoration of the home have to be solidly Islamic. "Orthopraxis" constitutes a convenient instrument for cultivating the distinction between oneself and "the other". The wearing of "Islamic dress", for example, aims at displaying Islamic identity and inviting recognition as such. These gestures become symbols marking the ethnic group (Barth 1994: 16). Not only external elements can be used to create distinctions; ideological differences can also serve that purpose.

They consider the familial praxis as prescribed by *Milli Görüs* as hugely different from that of their new country. Some of the girls in this study tried to live according to such Islamist values. Several girls adopted the "new" style without the approval of their mothers or fathers. They reproached their parents for not having been more conscientious in providing them with an "Islamic" upbringing. Claiming an Islamist identity became for some an instrument for distinguishing themselves from "loose" Belgian girls.

Militant Islamic movements attach a great deal of importance to the hierarchical, patriarchal relations within the family (Koçtürk 1992: 61). Felice Dassetto (1990: 201) speaks in this context of a familial re-socialisation to affirm the traditional roles. The dominant role of men is central to an Islamist frame of reference. The girls participating in the research had also been told that they should obey their male relatives. Not only older men, but younger ones, too, are urged to take more seriously their responsibility for female relatives and their duty to guard the women's moral behavior.

Young men, mostly "second generation", feel comfortable in an Islamist worldview. Especially the brothers of the girls involved in the study seemed attracted to it. Perhaps this is due to the fact that the immigration context is particularly harmful to the patriarchal role of young men in general (Kiray 1990). The socio-economic position of most young Turkish men is worse than that of their Belgian counterparts. They are generally not well educated and as a group are hit hard by unemployment. Even more so than women, they are targets of racism (Timmerman 1999). For these Muslim men who want to "re-legitimate" their male authority, the mosque may gain a new significance. Young Turkish immigrant men who are seeking a more prestigious status in society are gratified by the new social concern that the Islamist frame of reference has to offer (Timmerman 1994). Feeling insecure and searching for stability and a more positive identity elsewhere, they find solace in an Islamist ideology.

As we have already mentioned, young Turkish immigrant women are also increasingly choosing for an Islamist way of life. What makes a seemingly "misogynous" ideology so attractive to young urban girls?

Women: Central to the Image of Islam

Women appear to be central to the image of Islam. Although most people accept that Islam plays a significant role in the relationship between gender and politics in the Middle East, there is little agreement over its impact on the subservient position of women: "conservatives have used the Qur'an, the hadith and the lives of prominent women in the early period of Muslim history as sources to confirm that existing gender asymmetries are divinely ordained, while feminists have discerned possibilities for a more progressive politics of gender based on egalitarian ideal of early Islam" (Kandiyoti 1997: 185). This again demonstrates that, in the Middle East, Islam is the only legitimate framework for debating the social position of women. Today, there is a tendency even among secular feminists in the Middle East to start from a Muslim perspective – more specifically the ethical message of Islam – when advocating equality between husband and wife (Fawzi El-Solh and Mabro 1995: 17-19).

On the other hand, the Western image of women's place in Islamic society has been very negative for several decades: the Muslim woman is often perceived as a backward, oppressed and pitiful being whose lot is apparent from her veiled appearance. Clearly, this interest in the precarious position of the female in Islam should in part be seen as an instrument for justifying European colonialism and Western hegemony. In the Middle East, this has resulted in a closer association between feminism and Western cultural imperialism, which in turn has rendered feminism in this region culturally suspect (Kandiyoti 1991: 7).

The opposition against the colonial and Western view on women and Islam subsequently started to use the veil as a symbol of the dignity and validity of Islamic values and traditions. At a more general level, the woman and the family became the source of the Muslim identity and the area par excellence of cultural resistance. In other words, Western discourse itself gave new significance to the veil and the role of women in society and thus created the right conditions for it to become a "symbol of resistance" (Ahmed 1992: 164).

Also, one must not lose sight of the fact that, in the Islamic conscience, the Muslim family in general and a woman's maternal role in particular are regarded as the ideal of social solidarity (Eickelman and Piscatori 1996). The family is often perceived as a microcosm of the ideal moral order. As such, it can have important symbolic value. The family provides the perfect environment for men and women to fulfil their "natural" roles, whereby women are seen as the "mothers of the nation". In the same context, one notices that honoring the traditional domestic and familial role of women is often equated to retaining one's "authentic" ethnic identity (Eickelman and Piscatori 1996: 83-100). However, the significance that is attributed to cultural symbols as markers of the ethnic group diverges for the two sexes. Generally speaking, men can change and yet retain their authenticity, while the burden of continuity is placed upon the women. The scrutiny of their behavior is rarely proportional to the degree of integration and participation that they enjoy in society. As Delaney (1995: 190) puts it: "Women may symbolize the nation, but men represent it". It is up to women to keep intact the honor of the family, particularly its sexual honor.

As we have already pointed out, women are central to the social and moral order in the Middle East. Women appear to be the perfect embodiment of the dignity and authenticity of the (Islamic) nation. This carries with it a great responsibility, as any immoral or indecent behavior on the part of women is seen to reflect badly on society as a whole. On the other hand, this responsibility also has a positive side: if women are capable of exemplifying this symbolic value properly, they deserve great status.

Islamist movements organize many activities for girls and women: social and cultural events, meetings, courses and sports activities. Clearly, then, *Milli Görüs* pays a great deal of attention to catering for young girls and women. It is argued that later, when these women have become mothers, they will play a key role in the transmission of Islamist ideas. For permanent success, it is imperative that women are won over for their project. Young women are able to participate actively in social networks outside the familial context insofar as they meet the requirements of the Islamist social project. This implies obedience, even in public life, to the rules set by Islamism, including those governing the segregation of men and women and the covering of the female body.

As we have seen above, Islamist women attach a great deal of importance to dress. Islamic women's attire must, among other things, be sober and not in any way seductive. It offers practical benefits to women: it is cheaper than Western clothing, and it protects women against male harassment. Moreover, it gives young women a greater degree of social freedom: it makes it easier for them to interact with male colleagues or fellow-students without being branded as an "immoral" person. Through this style of dress, they are able to claim their own legitimate place in society outside the confines of the family. Women also use the headscarf as a means to escape from the traditional female environment and enter into the public domain (Ask and Tjomsland 1998: 12). Indeed, it is noticeable that the new style of clothing differs from Western attire as well as from traditional Islamic dress. Often it is an amalgamation of the two: "far from indicating that the wearers remain fixed in the world of tradition and the past, then, Islamist dress is the uniform of arrival, signalling entrance into, and determination to move forward in, modernity" (Ahmed 1992: 225).

The Islamization of Modernity

Many of the Turkish immigrant girls I met were not satisfied with their current situation; they felt they enjoyed only limited freedom of movement within the Turkish community. According to a "folk Islamic frame of reference" -- which is dominated by patrilineality and segregation of the sexes -- the social role of girls is situated within the family (Delaney 1991). This role is very clearly defined. Many of the girls felt they were being held hostage by this "folk" tradition, and that in order to escape this "limitation" they had to find a way of manifesting themselves outside the family context as defined by this folk Islamic worldview. In a Turkish context, education provides a legitimate alternative (Timmerman 2000). Within a Kemalist worldview, education is important for girls as well as for boys. Alongside the Islamic worldviews, which mainly emphasize women's role within the family, there exists another Turkish frame of reference that stresses the role of women in public life. The key to this emancipation is education. Turkish girls who "have studied" are regarded to have a legitimate reason to stand out within a Western-inspired frame of reference, and, in consequence, to develop personally outside the family context. It is not the contact with "Western culture" as such that makes the transition possible to a "Western" societal model, but successful participation in the school system.

However, the option of a Western-inspired way of life is problematic for many immigrant girls. In order to be able to justify such a "Western option" within their own community, certain conditions need to be fulfilled. Gaining high academic credentials or acquiring a high professional status is an essential criterion. Few immigrant girls are able to meet such requirements. By contrast, the criteria of Islamism – to observe orthopraxis and to accept the Islamic familial values as the basis for a just society – are within their reach. The participation of an individual in a movement depends on the presence and feasibility of other perspectives (Acar 1995: 64). The popularity of Islamist ideology is largely due to the absence of other appealing political movements that can serve as a basis for improving one's socio-cultural situation. In the eyes of many young girls, a militant Islamic movement such as *Milli Görüs* offers the most realistic prospect of improving one's self-esteem and one's socio-cultural position in the community.

Many Turkish migrant girls thus hope to improve their position by adhering to an Islamist way of life. The social reality of their daily existence seems to contradict the world with which they are confronted at school and in the media. This struggle with the contradictions of everyday life appears to be a central reason for women to adopt an Islamist perspective (Brenner 1996). To them, the choice for an Islamist frame of reference represents the best chance of escaping from these dilemmas and attaining a more comfortable social and economic position in Belgian society.

Another element making Islamism attractive is its unambiguous message. The ambiguity that exists in the confrontation of a Western and an Islamic value system is much smaller from an Islamist point of view than from a folk Islamic perspective.

When Tradition Becomes Fashionable: The Case of Young Turkish Women in Belgium

Questions about the desirability of certain Western conceptions simply become redundant. An Islamist vision – contrary to a folk Islamic frame of reference – formulates a clear and equally attractive alternative to the "Western model" (Toprak 1993: 255). As already mentioned, it does however incorporate many modern Western elements without regarding them as specifically Western. This is the case in education, technology, political and social organization, and even in personal behavior (Roy 1992). As Brenner asserts, Islamists want to be part of the modern world without the need to adopt a Westernized way of life (Brenner 1996: 678).

Ernest Gellner (1983: 76) feels that Islam is ideally prepared for a place in modern society because it is represented both in the "High Culture" (through orthodox Islam) and in the "Low Culture" (folk Islam). The high form of Islam has several characteristics that make it very suitable as a worldview in a modern urban environment: scripturalism, Puritanism, individualism, rule-orientation, a low loading of magic, an aversion to disorderly folk practices and mystical indulgence. As Acar (1995: 62) puts it: "It is hardly surprising that women born and raised in conservative settings, where the legitimacy of religious explanations has always been essentially unquestioned and Islamic values have loomed large in the background, should turn to Islamist recipes for self-esteem and happiness." The presence of a "tradition", i.e., folk Islam, that has great affinity with the "new" ideology, i.e., Islamism, makes the transition rather easy. This affinity offers advantages either way: to accommodate those people who are attached to "tradition", the links with the past can be stressed, while for those people who are attracted to "modernity", the opposition to local traditions can be emphasized.

Islamism is more adequately suited than secular nationalism to formulate answers to the existential questions of life. As other religious ideologies, it succeeds in giving meaning to profound human suffering, sickness, loss and death (Toprak 1987: 221). Secular worldviews are less successful in interpreting the often unacceptable conditions of human existence.

Conclusion

Turkish immigrants who settle in Belgium are confronted with a way of life that differs in many respects from the one they were accustomed to in their native country. Moreover, their children and grandchildren remain closely connected with Turkey and indeed define themselves firmly as Turks. Ethno-nationalism among Turkish immigrants is undoubtedly fuelled by the powerful patriotism, both secular and religious, that one encounters in Turkey itself. On the other hand, the way in which this nationalistic heritage is interpreted is influenced strongly by the concrete reality of the context of immigration. This is also the case among Turkish immigrant girls.

To many Turkish immigrants, so-called "tradition" offers a solid foundation for creating a "new" socio-cultural niche with which they can identify. Islam is an essential part of the cultural heritage of Turkish immigrants. As such, its more radical manifestation, Islamism, can offer an ideal frame of reference for coping with the often confusing situations created by a context of migration. The Islamist worldview is indeed gaining influence among the Turkish immigrant community of Belgium. Islamism has a number of characteristics that make it an attractive ideological frame for establishing a social project in a modern society.

For immigrant girls, who have little to hold on to socially, Islamism represents an unequivocal and all-embracing frame of reference that provides support. At the same time, the conditions that make Islam suitable as a discourse of protest against Western dominance contribute to the popularity of Islamism. In other words, a context of unredeemed expectations and frustrations adds to the appeal of an ideology, i.e., Islamism, that promises justice on the basis of a familiar worldview, i.e., Islam. Furthermore, the fact that women are central to the image of Islam gives young urban immigrant girls possibilities for acquiring a positive and esteemed identity. Females are seen to symbolize the cultural authenticity expressed in Islamic terms. The impact of the Western image on the creation of the woman as a symbol of authenticity and cultural resistance within an Islamic discourse cannot be denied. In Islamism, women are regarded as the embodiment of Islamic originality and as such they have a great symbolic value in distinguishing Islamic society from the West.

Endnotes

[1] "Ethnic Identity" is defined as "the feeling of belonging and continuity in existence" constituted by "self- or other- ascription" and "which claims common ancestors and cultural tradition " (Roosens 1994).

[2] C. Timmerman, S. Balli, I. Lodewyckx, and K. Van der Heyden, Integratie van tweede generatie migrantenvrouwen in Vlaanderen: verschillende wegen tot integratie. Onderzoek uitgevoerd door de Onderzoeksgroep Armoede, Sociale Uitsluiting en

Minderheden in opdracht van het Ministerie van de Vlaamse Gemeenschap, Gelijke Kansen in Vlaanderen. Antwerpen: UFSIA – Universiteit Antwerpen, 1999. 42 (+ bijlagen).

[3] C. Timmerman, C., K. Van der Heyden, Y. Ben Abdeljelil, and J. Geets, Marokkaanse en Turkse nieuwkomers in Vlaanderen. Onderzoek uitgevoerd door de Onderzoeksgroep Armoede, Sociale Uitsluiting en Stad in opdracht van het Ministerie van de Vlaamse Gemeenschap voor Welzijn, Gezondheid en Gelijke Kansen. Antwerpen: UFSIA – Universiteit Antwerpen, 2000. 225 (+ bijlagen).

[4] The term "second generation" refers to children of immigrants who were born in the host country, in this case Belgium.

[5] In this context J. Kellas speaks of "reform nationalism". The initial purpose of this sort of nationalism was national rebirth. It was however limited to the existing state. Nationalists – in the first place Atatürk – were those who already governed the state. With reform they hoped for economic modernization and they strove for independence of foreign control and the defense of national identity. They overthrew European imperialists and established a modern nation state. According to Kellas, this kind of nationalism expressed itself especially in antipathy towards foreigners and in the promotion of the national language and culture. (J. Kellas, *The Politics of Nationalism and Ethnicity London*: Macmillan Education LTD, 1991: 75).

[6] In Belgium there are other Turkish Islamic movements besides *Milli Görüs*, but they are all less prominent. An example is the *Süleymancilar*, which was founded in 1973 in Germany. In the 1980s, their network encompassed 150 mosques and 300 local organizations in the European Community. The *Naksibendi* and the *Nurcu* movements are also active in Belgium (Leman 1992).

Works Cited

Acar, F. "Women and Islam in Turkey." *Women in Modern Turkish Society: A Reader.* Ed. S. Tekeli. London: Zed, 1995: 46-65.

Ahmed, A. " 'Ethnic Cleansing': A Metaphor for Our Time?" *Ethnic and Racial Studies* 18 (1995): 26-45.

Ahmed, L. *Women and Gender in Islam. Historical Roots of a Modern Debate.* New Haven, London: Yale UP, 1992.

Ask, K., and M. Tjomsland. *Women and Islamization. Contemporary Dimensions of Discourse on Gender Relations.* Oxford, New York: Berg, 1998.

Atalik, G., and B. Beeley. "What Mass Migration Has Meant for Turkey." *Mass Migration in Europe. The Legacy and the Future.* Ed. K. Russell. London: Belhaven, 1992: 156-173.

Badran, M. "Competing Agenda: Feminists, Islam and the State in the 19th and 20th Century Egypt." *Women, Islam and the State.* Ed. D. Kandiyoti. London: Macmillan, 1991: 201-236.

Barth, F., ed. *Ethnic Groups and Boundaries. The Social Organization of Culture Difference.* Oslo: Scandinavian UP, 1969.

---. "Enduring and Emerging Issues in the Analysis of Ethnicity." *The Anthropology of Ethnicity. Beyond "Ethnic Groups and Boundaries."* Eds. H. Vermeulen and C. Govers. Amsterdam: Het Spinhuis, 1994: 11-32.

Bayar, A. "Un ghetto du travail. Les nettoyeuses turques à Bruxelles." *Les femmes et la ville.* Ed. E. Gubin. Bruxelles: Editions Labour, 1993: 213-225.

Bilgrami, A. "What is a Muslim? Fundamental Commitment and Cultural Identity." *Critical Inquiry* 18 (1992): 821-842.

Brenner, S. "Reconstructing Self and Society: Javanese Muslim Women and the Veil." *American Ethnologist: Journal of the American Ethnological Society* 4 (1996): 673-697.

Cakir, R. "La mobilisation islamique en Turquie." *Esprit* août-septembre (1992): 130-142.

Cizre-Sakallioglu, Ü. "Kemalism, Hyper-Nationalism and Islam in Turkey." *History of European Ideas* 18 (1994): 255-270.

Dassetto, F. "Visibilisation de l'Islam dans l'espace public." *Immigrations et nouveaux pluralismes. Une confrontation de sociétés.* Eds. A. Bastenier and F. Dassetto. Bruxelles: De Boeck-Wesmael, 1990: 179-208.

Delaney, C. *The Seed and the Soil. Gender and Cosmology in Turkish Village Society.* Berkeley: U of California P, 1991.

---. "Father State, Motherland, and the Birth of Modern Turkey." *Naturalizing Power.* Eds. S. Yanagisako and C. Delaney. New York; London: Routledge, 1995: 177-199.

Eickelman, D., and J. Piscatori. *Muslim Politics.* Princeton: Princeton UP, 1996.

Fawzi El-Solh, C., and J. Mabro. *Muslim's Women Choices. Religious Belief and Social Reality.* Providence, Oxford: Berg, 1995.

Gellner, E. *Nations and Nationalism.* Oxford: Blackwell, 1983.

---. *Conditions of Liberty. Civil Society and Its Rivals.* New York: Penguin, 1994.

Juergensmeyer, M. *The New Cold War? Religious Nationalism Confronts the Secular State.* Berkeley, Los Angeles, Oxford: U of California P (2), 1993.

Kandiyoti, D. "Introduction". *Women, Islam and the State.* Ed. D. Kandiyoti. London: Macmillan, 1991: 1-21.

---. "End of Empire: Islam, Nationalism and Women in Turkey." *Women, Islam and the State.* Ed. D. Kandiyoti. London: Macmillan, 1991: 22-47.

---. "Women, Islam, and the State." *Political Islam. Essays from Middle East Report.* Eds. J. Beinin and J. Stork. Berkeley, Los Angeles: U of California P, 1997: 185-193.

Kellas, J. *The Politics of Nationalism and Ethnicity.* London: Macmillan Education LTD, 1991.

Kiray, M. "Changing Patterns of Patronage: A Study in Structural Change." *Sex Roles, Family, and Community in Turkey.* Ed. C. Kagitcibasi. Bloomington, Indiana: Indiana University Turkish Studies, 1982: 269-297.

---. "The Family of the Migrant Worker." *Women, Family and Social Change in Turkey.* Ed. F. Ozbay. Bangkok: UNESCO, 1990: 72-93.

Koçtürk, T. *A Matter of Honour. Experiences of Turkish Women Immigrants.* London, New Jersey: Zed Books, 1992.

Lindholm, C. "Prophets and Pirs: Charismatic Islam in the Middle East and South Asia." *Embodying Charisma. Modernity, Locality and the Performance of Emotion in Sufi Cults.* Eds. P. Werbner and H. Basu. London, NewYork: Routledge: 1998. 209-233.

MacLeod, A. "Hegemonic Relations and Gender Resistance: The New Veiling as Accomodating Protest in Cairo." *Signs* 3 (1992): 533-557.

Manço, A., and U. Manço. "Turcs de Belgique: portrait d'une immigration." *Turcs de Belgique. Identités et trajectoires d'une minorité.* Eds. A. Manço and U. Manço. Bruxelles: Info-Türk, 1992: 27-43.

Manço, U. "L'avenir des minorités originaires de Turquie dans la Communauté européenne." *Turcs de Belgique. Identités et trajectoires d'une minorité.* Eds. A. Manço and U. Manço. Bruxelles: Info-Türk, 1992: 227-279.

Meeker, M. "Oral Culture, Media Culture and the Islamic Resurgence in Turkey." *Exploring the Written in Anthropology.* Ed. E. Archetti. Oslo: Scandinavian UP, 1994: 31-63.

Onis, Z. "The Political Economy of Islamic Resurgence in Turkey: The Rise of the Welfare Party in Perspective." *Third World Quarterly* 18 (1997): 743-766.

Poulain, M. *Migrations en Belgique. Données démographiques. Courrier hebdomadaire n° 1438-1439.* Bruxelles: CRISP, 1994.

Ross, J. "Politics, Religion, and Ethnic Identity in Turkey." *Religion and Politics in the Middle East.* Ed. M. Curtis. Boulder, Colorado: Westview, 1981.

Roy, O. "L'échec de l'islam politique." *Esprit* août-septembre (1992): 106-129.

Sivan, E. "The Islamic Resurgence: Civil Society Strikes Back." *Fundamentalism in Comparative Perspective.* Ed. L. Kaplan. Amherst: U of Massachusetts P, 1992: 96-108.

Smith, A. *The Ethnic Origins of Nations.* Oxford: Blackwell, 1986.

Tapper, R. *Islam in Modern Turkey. Religion, Politics and Literature in a Secular State.* London, New York: I.B. Tauris, 1991.

Timmerman, C. "Jeunes filles de Turquie: Vie familiale et instruction scolaire." *Familles turques et maghrébines aujourd'hui. Evolution dans les espaces d'origine et d'immigration.* Ed. N. Bensalah. Paris: Maisonneuve et Larose, 1994: 175-188.

---. *Onderwijs maakt het verschil. Socio-culturele praxis en etniciteitsbeleving bij jonge Turkse vrouwen. Drie perspectieven.* Leuven: Acco, 1999.

---. "Secular and Religious Nationalism among Young Turkish Women in Belgium: Education May Make the Difference." *Anthropology and Education Quarterly* 3 (2000): 333-354.

Toprak, B. "The Religious Right." *Turkey in Transition. New Perspectives.* Eds. C. Schick and E. Tonak. New York, Oxford: Oxford UP, 1987: 218-235.

---. "Islamist Intellectuals: Revolt against Industry and Technology." *Turkey and the West. Changing Political and Cultural Identities.* Eds. M. Heper, A. Öncü and H. Kramer. London, New York: Tauris, 1993: 237-257.

Van Nieuwenhuijze, C. "Islamism-A Defiant Utopianism." *Die Welt des Islams* 35 (1995): 1-36.

Zürcher, E. *Turkey. A Modern History*. London, New York: I. B. Tauris, 1993.

Responses to Migration in Italy: Social Integration and Representations of the "Immigrant"

Mariangela Veikou

Migration is now seen as a major feature of social structure, personal identity and often political conflict. It is seen by some as challenging existing social hierarchies and oppressive conceptions of citizenship, and by others as introducing a new tribalism in society that threatens democracy and economic development. Given its increasing prominence in contemporary socio-political debates, studies on migration address a variety of issues in social science disciplines. Among the different disciplines and approaches there are some case-studies that appear to be more "typical" than others. More specifically, migration studies in Europe provide us with discussions concerning the actual and potential implications of migration for the European states but, often, the examples they bring concentrate predominantly on the long experience of northern European (EU) societies with migration. Yet, the modalities of immigrant integration in Southern European (EU) societies and the societal transformations reflecting the increased "visibility" of migrants within them are obviously experienced quite differently. This paper attempts to address the difference of experiences in the context of southern Europe by presenting a case-study from Italy, which is a European country with a fairly recent experience with immigration.

The paper is based on research conducted during the years 2000-1 in Italy, in the framework of an international project funded by the European Commission, which concentrated on making sense of Europe's immigrant receiving societies (Italy, Greece, Germany and the UK).1 Data from interview-texts gathered during that period are analysed anew in the present paper, to examine and reflect on the representations of the "immigrant" in Italian society as revealed by the daily practices of two agencies involved with the implementation of the immigration law provisions. In the section that follow the background of immigration policy implementation in Italy is presented. Attention is paid to the main provisions regulating immigrant (non-EU nationals) stay permits (issue and renewal) for work purposes as well as to the institutional actors and bureaucratic procedures involved in their implementation.

The Immigration Policy Framework

Italy discovered itself to be a country of immigration since the beginning of the 1980s, without yet having comprehensive immigration policies. Throughout the 1980s, there was a big number of immigrants from Africa, Asia and Eastern Europe arriving in Italy because of the country's sudden economic growth and the near absence of immigration controls at that time.

In the Italian political debate on immigration (as well as in the media and even at times in scholarly debates) the issue, then, was characterized as a "social emergency". A number of matters arose in relation to immigrants, i.e., their social accommodation, informal labor, political asylum. There was poor delivery of social services, housing problems, problematic management of the labor market (a particularly large underground economy) with the immigrants engaging in low-paying, temporary, irregular employment. Only in 1986 the state introduced an immigration law into the legislation to regulate conditions for admission, stay, expulsion and prohibition of entry at the border (Reyneri 1999; Bonifaci 2000). Though elaborate, the law was not comprehensive in terms of principles and provisions for its implementation.

In 1989, because of pressures from northern European countries in view to the implementation of the Schengen agreements, a new law was prepared. It made the conditions for entry into the country more strict and introduced amnesty programs for the regularization of those already present in the country. The turnout of the first amnesty program was relatively low, hence, five (in total) amnesty programs were introduced in fifteen years from 1986 to 2001 (1986, 1990, 1996, 1998 and 2001).

The most recent legislation on immigration policy is Law 48/1998 (Testo unico delle disposizioni concernenti la disciplina dell'immigrazione e norme sulla condizione dello straniero – Unique text of legal dispositions concerning immigration and norms regarding the condition of foreigners). It gave an impetus to the debate about immigrant integration and control measures (Veikou and Triandafyllidou, 2001). It came to put an end to the emergency-based approach to migration management by combining immigration control and integration policies into a stable policy framework. It is effective in positive ways, in particular with provisions regarding stay and work conditions, family reunion, as well as with efforts for the social integration of immigrants that already reside in the country. Nevertheless, a number of problematic aspects are identified. For instance, there are regulations that are guided by a popular discourse on migration as an imminent threat.

This study examines the regulation of immigrants' entry into the Italian labor market and society. Studying the specific policy measures, namely the issue and renewal of stay permits for work purposes, it offers a useful case study for research which aims at achieving a better understanding of the institutional and cultural mechanisms that lie behind immigrants' integration into the Italian society. Looking at the implementation of legal provisions and administrative decisions allowed us to examine the representations of immigrants in the daily practices of institutions charged with the specific aspect of immigrants' integration, i.e., the regulation of immigrant labor. Employment is one of the main reasons for which foreigners (non EU nationals) are allowed entry and stay into the country (see table 1). One of the principal objectives of the Italian immigration policy is to regulate foreign labor. This is achieved by setting and applying annual caps that are set at the national level and further specified regionally in collaboration with regional authorities. National as well as regional actors are involved in deciding how implementation is carried out. The regulations and resources for regional activities are comprised within the more general framework of national legislation. The design of implementation is based on an ideal of a neutral and competent civil service (against popular opinions that observe favouritism/discretion in the Italian civil service) which has efficiency as its guiding principle.

The overall economic structure of Italy, with its large underground economy, as well as the change in the administration in Italy, during the period 1999-2001 (the years covered by this study) are factors of high importance implicated in the way immigration policy is implemented in the country.[2] Before presenting the legal directives and administrative procedures concerning the stay permits as well as the main actors, both institutional and non-governmental, involved, let me interject information on the general features and new standards of the Italian public administration.

Italian Administration in Transition

The years 1999 to 2000 was a period of transition for the Italian administration. The national administration has undergone few changes in its essential characteristics for almost half a century. Its institutional capacity in the past, especially with regard to the performance of the public administration, has been considered to be substantially lower than that of other Western democracies. In recent years attention has focused on reform of institutions, including the public administration and civil service management (Lewanski, 1999:97).

Central and local government reform processes, and, as a consequence, the restructuring of bureaucracy can be interpreted as responses to the Italian state's need for legitimacy. The centralized administration that governed the relationship between the regions and the nation-state was based, and to a certain extent still is, on the clientele system. In a clientelistic system particular segments of the political system have special relations with particular groups of the population. The latter will assure their consensus to the extent to which the former are able to satisfy their particularistic needs and demands (Dente 1995:175). The division of tasks between politicians (responsible for the formation of policies) and the civil service (in charge of their implementation) in fact did not result in transparency of tasks.

The national, political and administrative system underwent two major legitimization crises – the first during the 1960s and 1970s and the second one during the 1980s and 1990s – which signaled the urgent need for modernization. Below I will present the main issues raised in the reforms and the main features of the Italian administration in the transitional period.

The highly centralized state (in spite of its formal division in 17 regions since 1948) hampered the administrative efficiency of regional authorities. Demands for reforms in the 1960-70s focused on the introduction of more democratic procedures in the political and administrative system. In the 1980-90s there was a critical political period with disruptive consequences for the public administration (i.e., the Tangentopoli scandals in 1992 exposed the widespread corruption and favouritism in Italian politics and public administration at the national level). In that political context, the poor performance of the administration contributed to the de-legitimization of the entire institutional system (Gilbert 1995:90).

The process of administrative reform was advanced under the governments of Giuliano Amato (1992-3), Carlo Azeglio Ciampi (1993-4), and Romano Prodi (1996-8). The latter set up three laws for a drastic reform: Laws 59/1997; 127/1997 and 191/1998. They introduced provisions for the decentralization of the civil service and simplified bureaucratic procedures partly by clearly distancing the politics and the administration. The so-called "administrative federalism" transferred considerable powers to regional authorities. In brief, the reform concentrated in the following main aspects of organizational management:

- A process called "privatization" by was installed which the employees of the public sector become subject to the same conditions, guarantees and obligations as those in the private sector.
- Relevant jurisdiction was transferred from the administrative courts to public courts (Lewanski 1999: 117).
- Public exams were introduced to increase the transparency in the recruitment procedures.
- New flexible use of human resources work were allowed.
- Clientalism was targeted by autonomous decision making of high ranking employees of high professional competence and status in administrative offices. Top managers were to be hired on the basis of private law contracts responsible for administrative management (Dente 1997:183).
- Importance was assigned to the improvement of the relations between citizens (and clients in general) and public employees. To these effects, reception desks have been established as well as public relations offices to facilitate client access to administration.

The administrative reform enacted in Italy the last few years discloses current features of the Italian administrative culture in general, which determine, as revealed by the study, the organizational culture in the specific agencies this study concentrates on. Below we can see the administrative procedure followed concerning the issue/renewal of stay permits for work purposes and the actors involved.

Entry and Residence in Italy

All foreigners who wish to regularize their position in Italy should appear at the Foreigners' Office (*Ufficio Stranieri*) of the provincial Police Headquarters (*Questura*) with the relevant documents to apply for a residence permit (D.P.C.M., 24.10.98).

Residence permit (permesso di soggiorno): To get a residence permit a foreigner must apply to the Questura of the Italian province in which s/he wishes to reside, within eight working days of the date of entry into Italy (note: When a foreigner is already in Italy, s/he cannot apply for the extension of a visa; s/he can only apply for an extension or renewal of her/his residence permit, provided that her/his visa documents are still valid) presenting a passport and financial documents (an attestation of sufficient means for return to the home country). The Questura may ask for alternative documents to support the request of a residence permit. For example, for stateless persons or if there is no passport, another document equivalent to the passport (a travel document, laisser passer or identity declaration by the Embassy or Consulate) can be accepted. The *Questura* may also ask for evidence stating the foreigner's date of entry into Italy.

When the *Questura* files the application, a receipt is given to the applicant, which is not to be considered a residence permit. The period of time allowed by the residence permit is the same as that stated by the foreigner's entry visa. This period cannot be longer than three months for visit, business or tourism, six to nine months for temporary work visas, a year (renewable) for study visas, and two years for freelance work, subordinate employment or family reunification. A residence permit or its renewal can be refused or cancelled when the conditions for entry or residence in Italy are no longer valid. The conditions for issuing or renewing a permit vary in relation to the activities it has been issued for.

Conversion of residence permit: A residence permit obtained for work or family reasons allows the permit holder to carry out the activities specified (article 6, law 40/1998). A permit can be modified according to the activity actually carried out; a study permit, for instance, before its expiration, can be changed into a work permit, within the yearly immigration quotas. A permit to work as an employee can be transformed into a permit to work freelance when a foreigner has the prescribed licence. A permit to work freelance enables foreigners to work as employees, after registration in an employment list or after the employer has notified the Provincial Employment Office. A family residence permit enables foreigners to work.

Renewal of residence permit: A residence permit can be renewed by request to the *Questura*, at least thirty days before expiration and after the conditions for extension have been checked as valid (article 5 of law 40/1998). In order to renew a foreigner's permit, the foreigner's income, deriving from lawful actions, has to be officially assessed as being sufficient to support the applicant and dependent relatives.

Expulsion: For reasons of public policy and/or national safety, the Prefecture (*Prefettura*) can order the expulsion of the foreigner that extends her/his stay in Italian territory after the eight days provided by the law, without having initiated the procedure for the residence permit request (articles 18 and 19 of Law 40/1998).

Institutional Actors

The institutional agencies involved in the issue and renewal of stay permits are the following:

- The Foreigners' Office of the *Questura*: The Questura is the provincial headquarters of the national police force; it deals with issues of public security and the "fight against crime". It belongs to the operational structure of the Ministry of Interior. The Foreigners' Office of the *Questura* controls and regulates the stay and work of foreigners; it is responsible for the issue and renewal of the related permits. The Foreigners' Office of each *Questura* is divided into two sections. The "sojourn" section (*sezione soggiorni*) that manages the stay and work of immigrants and the "expulsion" section (*sezione expulsioni*), which deals with enforcement and expulsion orders (Quassoli and Chiodi, 2000).

- The Prefecture (*Prefettura*) forms part of the Ministry of the Interior but not of the Police. It is the administrative and policy branch of this Ministry concerning public security. The Prefecture is functionally superior to the *Questura* although this last holds the operational power.

- Immigration Office of the Municipality (*Ufficio Immigrati del Comune*): Many municipalities have an immigration office which functions as a reference center proving information to employers (potential and actual) and occasionally to immigrants concerning work or accommodation.

- Provincial Labor Office (*Ufficio Provinciale del Lavoro*): This is the provincial branch of the Ministry of Labor in charge of (a) labor policy (labor policy office) and (b) management of the labor market and more particularly labor inspections (labor inspection office). The office inspecting the labor market is also responsible for issuing the employment booklet (*libretto di lavoro*) that any worker is obliged to have in order to be legally employed. This office also performs checks as to whether employers and employees are conforming to the legal requirements with regard to work contracts.

- Employment Office (*Ufficio di Collocamento per l'Impiego*): These agencies are organized into local, neighborhood offices responsible for (a) the registration of job seekers onto employment lists, and (b) the eventual allocation of the available jobs.

Non-Governmental Actors

- Voluntary Associations (*Associazioni di volontariato*): These include NGOs, religious organizations and immigrant associations with immigrant and Italian members. They provide general assistance and information to immigrant workers and their families.

- Accommodation Centers (*Centri di Accoglienza*): These are centers that provide housing and social assistance to immigrants while they also have a function of patrolling immigrant people, temporary residing therein. They generally host only a limited number of immigrants for short periods of time.

Regulating Immigrant Labor

A foreigner who applies for the issue or renewal of a stay permit for employed work has to produce the following documents issued by different offices and submit them to the *Questura* with her/his application: (a) passport; (b) date of entry; (c) regularization application; (d) stay permit; (e) employment registration; (f) contract; (g) employment booklet; (h) tax code; (i) residence registration; (k) rent contract; (l) statement of suitable accommodation (see table 2).

The Law also makes conditions clearer as to what is required by an immigrant in order to reside in Italy legally. Workers can enter and stay in Italy through the following procedures: the national seasonal quotas; the work contracts with an Italian employer; and availing of the "sponsorship" of an Italian resident. To those immigrants a temporary permit can be issued within a planned quota. There are two main categories of permits for work purposes: those issued for dependent employment, and those allowing for self-employment. The procedure to be followed in each case differs.

a. Stay Permit for Dependent Employment: Concerning dependent employment, the official procedure comprises of the following steps: the employer presents an official request to the Provincial Labor Office in order to acquire the job offer authorization (*autorizzazione al lavoro offerto*). This authorization is granted only if the specific job is within the regional immigration quota, as these are defined by the government in the beginning of each calendar year. The request has to specify the type and place of employment, the name of the employer and of the potential employee, and the availability of suitable accommodation for the immigrant worker. Once the job offer authorization is obtained, the employer presents it to the local *Questura* and applies for an entry authorization (*autorizzazione all' ingresso*) for the immigrant. The *Questura* checks whether there are any particular motives for refusing entry to this immigrant (penal claims) and issues a job authorization. Then the job offer authorization is sent via the Italian Embassy or Consulate to the immigrant in her/his country of origin. The consular authorities are thus able to issue an entrance visa for the specific individual enabling her/him to undertake employment in Italy under the conditions specified in the offer.

Within eight days of her/his entry to Italy, the foreign employee has to report personally to the *Questura* and apply for a stay permit for dependent employment submitting the relevant documents. Within five days of the immigrant's entry the employer has to declare the initiation of the contract s/he previously offered to the immigrant in the Provincial Labor Office and request by the Labor Inspection Office the employment booklet where welfare contributions paid in favor of the immigrant are registered. The employment booklet stays with the employer for the duration of the specific contract. If the contract is terminated, the employment booklet is returned to the immigrant so that s/he may take up another position.

b. Stay Permit for Self-Employment: The foreigner who wishes to come to Italy in search for a job has to register with the lists of potential immigrant workers in the Italian Embassy or Consulate at her/his country of origin. S/he also has to demonstrate through bank statement or other documents that s/he has sufficient economic means to support himself/herself while searching for a job in Italy. Alternatively, s/he has to contact personally the relevant administrative authority, usually the Chamber of Commerce (or other trade or professional association) of the specific town or province where s/he aims to settle, to ask for permission to exercise her/his profession. The Chamber of Commerce sends a declaration which specifies that there are no objections to the Chamber of Commerce's issuing a certificate that the specific applicant may initiate the economic activity s/he wishes to undertake. The certificate attesting that the immigrant may undertake the specific profession or activity is submitted to the *Questura*. As in the case of dependent employment, the immigrant has to apply personally to the *Questura* of the locality where s/he will reside for a stay permit for *self-employment*.

c. The "Sponsorship" Option: An important innovation of the law concerns the provision about Italian resident citizens guaranteeing and supporting immigrants looking for a job. The "sponsorship" option is an alternative route of entry for immigrants seeking employment in Italy who have neither a concrete job offer by a specific employer nor sufficient means to support themselves while seeking for a job. An immigrant may obtain a one-year stay permit for work purposes if an Italian individual or family or a trade union or voluntary association accept to "sponsor" him/her. The "sponsor" has to bring proof (bank statements and/or municipality certificates) that s/he possesses the necessary economic means to support the immigrant and will provide suitable accommodation for her/him during that year.

The "guarantee", signed by the sponsor, is submitted to the *Questura*. In the case of associations "sponsoring" more than one immigrant worker – there is a maximum limit of two individuals sponsored by an individual and six by an organization, provided that they satisfy the economic means requested by the law – a list of the names of foreigners for whom a guarantee is provided has to be submitted too. The *Questura* then issues the entry authorization which has to be sent to the immigrant through the Italian consular authorities in her/his country, within sixty days from when it was granted by the *Questura*. The consular authorities are then able to issue a visa for work purposes enabling the specific worker to enter Italy and search for employment.

Unemployed immigrants also have to register with the Local Employment Office to be inserted in the job lists. The employment policy followed by these offices includes a placement program, which involves the listing of job openings with the aim of matching job seekers with job openings reported to the Employment Office by employers. Job listings may come from public or private employers locally, regionally or nationally. The task of identifying job seekers is restricted to waiting for people to walk into the Employment Office.

Research Design: The Case Study and Methodology

The empirical part of the research was conducted in the institutional environment related to the implementation of immigration policies in Florence, Italy. Florence, capital of Tuscany region, presents a sizeable immigrant population. In 1999 Tuscany accounted for just below 90.000 stay permits, of which over 50.000 were issued in Florence. In the same year there were 1.2 million immigrants (documented) present in Italy (Caritas 1999). We studied the organizational culture of one institutional actor – the Foreigner Office of the Police Headquarters (*Questura*) – and one non-governmental actor – an Accommodation Center (*Centro di Accoglienza*) – involved in the implementation of immigration law in Florence. The aim was to study the synchronic aspects of culture manifested in talk, values, beliefs of the people therein. Against this knowledge we hoped to reveal various themes in the representation of immigrants in this framework of employee/agent versus client/immigrant context of relation. The analysis is based on data collected by means of participant observation and unstructured interviews with public employees and migrants. The immigrant group on which the study has particularly focus, were the Albanians, the second largest immigrant group in Italy, but immigrants from other country backgrounds were also considered (i.e., Serbians). This group of immigrants is the one most frequently and most negatively represented in the Italian public discourse.

Access to the field of research was not easy. In the case of the *Questura* a written authorization of entry for the purposes of the research had to be obtained by the head of the police in Florence before we were allowed to establish contact with any of the agents in the office. While this authorization enabled us to visit the physical premises of the office, actual interviews with individual agents were arranged after renewed authorizations and letter requests. Contacts and interviews with individual police officers serving at the *Questura* were conducted in the premises during or just after their working hours. Generally, it was felt that access varied a lot, depending on the individual employee of higher / lower rank, on the supervising officer to permit interviews and observation of work practices. The formality of the authorization was generally seen positively also from other, separate agencies. The written authorization obtained by the police headquarters served to facilitate access to the accommodation center, although it belonged to a different service, regardless of their reluctance "in principle" to permit interviews, as we were told. Most of the immigrants contacted in the accommodation center were willing to be interviewed. During the first meeting, when appointments were to be arranged for the interviews, the social worker of the center was present. This did not seem to seriously inhibit contact, and the lack of availability in some cases was due to work schedules and their non-fixed work routines. Few of them refused to give an interview. As regards the setting of the interviews, they were always conducted within the center, in a private room, next to the office of the security agent.

Interviews were loosely structured around a set of themes (see table 3) which were raised during the interviews/discussions randomly, following the flow of the interview. Data was additionally gathered via participant observation, and field notes had been kept.

The approach adopted for the analysis of the interview texts was that of discourse analysis. Attention was paid to the interactions between "agents" and "clients" as well as their individual narratives on the following dimensions: formal and informal practice codes; goals and aims of the agency; work conditions and work style; ritual or conventional language practice when addressing clients (see table 4); personal or impersonal authority; structure of authority and hierarchy; work load; supervisory style; and individual and professional values.

Findings: Representation of Immigrants

The Foreigners' Office, which deals with issues of entry, stay, residence and work permits, forms part of the provincial *Carabinieri* (armed police force) Police Headquarters. This easily links up with the popular belief that undocumented immigrant residence and criminal behavior go hand in hand. It is striking that in legal documents the undocumented status is referred to as "illegality" (*illegalita*). Additionally, the special Accommodation Centers (C*entri di Accoglienza*) appear to function, in effect, quite alike to detention centers; though directed by voluntary associations they are patrolled by security agents. It is a control measure: immigrants after several months of stay as "guests" (*hospiti*) in these centers are invited to make sure they have either employment or sponsorship in Italy, or, alternatively, they must return to their home countries. It is very revealing of the general Italian perception about immigrants that the amnesty programs in everyday colloquial language are called "Sanatoria" (catholic health centers subsidized by the state for the physically and mentally ill poor), which actually implies that via these programs the immigrants emerge from a state of social illness to a socially healthy condition of being regularized.

During the 1990s the Albanian immigration to Italy was constructed as an heroic event – the rhetoric was about fellow European people escaping the hardship of communism – but soon after, the public reaction was far from enthusiastic and the construction of the Albanian immigration changed, assuming "racial" elements. The Albanians became either "people of a bad race" (*razza cattiva*) or they were rejected as criminals. In some interviews, the narratives demonstrate the association made between the fact that the Albanian immigrants are more likely to arrive to the country with an undocumented status and the generalizations about the character, implying the "race", of the people. So the Albanians are represented as the dangerous immigrants par excellence – violent, corrupted by the authoritarian Albanian regime (former) and unsuitable for labor.

Concerning the issue of access to employment, interviewees reported that access to jobs are conditioned by networks and contacts. They were living under very difficult conditions, afraid to be arrested and repatriated. Ironically, an undocumented status opens up the possibility to find a job in Italy's sizeable underground economy, of course under hard working conditions, long working hours and low salaries. The immigrants who entered Italy with no valid documents are aware of the need to have regular documents. In order to regularize their position, they have to apply to the *Sanatoria* after convincing employers to help them obtain legal status. But relations with employers proved to be particularly stressful and tricky. The interviewees reported that they were treated with prejudice and that few employers offer to pay the welfare benefits that would entitle the immigrant to apply for a work permit. Furthermore, the procedure for applying for regularization is complicated for immigrants as well as for employers, who often do not spare the time and the effort.

About the daily routines of implementation practices at the *Questura*, direct contact between employees and immigrants is influenced by local sense-making value behavior. The equality of treatment and non-discrimination is a value well repeated in the office: "…we treat each individual regardless of nationality in the same manner … all protected by the law… because the immigrant is facing a lot of pressure… and for the immigrant the permit is life". Nonetheless, the equality before the law value, a humanitarian argument, is also raised. Their spirit of public service is often related to their conviction that the immigrants are people in need, facing particular hardship because they are in a foreign country. At times this takes the form of "organized philanthropy": individual police agents put special initiative and agency into serving specific clients whom they perceive as being in special need. Discretionary practices involving more flexible interpretation of the law aim to find solutions in daily routine and appear to hide a network of power relations. The perception of social distance is behind these charitable attitudes based on assumptions and pre-existing stereotypes of the "needy immigrant". The need to emphasize the proper conduct of the agents despite the workload reveals a rather ambiguous interplay between a politically correct discourse and an underlying categorization of immigrants in terms of ethnicity and related ethnic identity: "…I start with the presupposition that when the Italians, Americans, Africans, whatever, going to a foreign country they face problems (…) numerous (…) A Chinese for example when getting his permit thanks the officer a hundred times, but say, an Albanian being said that something is not possible, he hits the counter's window. (…) This makes part of the temperament of the person".

Quite similarly, in the context of the accommodation center and concerning internal controls as well as the confrontation with the police, immigrants discussed the Italian hypocrisy of organized philanthropy and ethnic prejudices. Furthermore, they stated that they felt deprived of opportunities to create a social life outside of the group in the accommodation center and to establish relationships and personal contacts that would help overcome the negative stereotypes and prejudices. Concerning the immigrants' contacts with the employees at the *Questura*, the interviewees found the Italian bureaucracy very complicated and controversial. They reported that work was arbitrary and that the practice in the office depended on the specific agent's interpretation of the law.

Interestingly, in spite of the "public mission" of the agents/employees, one way to handle loaded work pressure was a type of coded language. Language expressions become a tool for the agents to control work routine and problems and verbally manage tight work schedules (see table 4). Such language codes were few, simple typified expressions which were repeated frequently to deal with a variety of (mostly uncertain) circumstances like complex cases, tension, contradictions and information on new circulars and decisions. Through language employees construct common understandings, "legitimize" their practices among themselves, impel certain complications and facilitate circumstances.

Some immigrants emphasized the importance of "acquaintances" when dealing with the agents. The presence of Italian lawyers employed by the immigrants in mediating between the immigrant and the agent in the *Questura* is frequent, also because most of the clients did not speak good Italian. The relationships between employees and clients was significantly characterized by the "foreigner-ness" of the latter. The fact that the client was a "foreigner" (*lo straniero*, a non-Italian) was observed to be salient: "…It is in a person's character... we are human beings, and it may happen that one can get upset with the foreigner but it is also a cultural question involved. If one does not speak Italian it does not mean that this person is an idiot... it is a cultural matter". The immigrants themselves claimed the institutional environment they are subjected to occasionally makes them feel unsafe, uncertain and exposes them as "victims". In fact, they reject any victimization, or cultural and ethnic explanations in making sense of their migration experience, and they attribute responsibility to the political system and complex bureaucratic procedures.

All the above reveal interesting patterns and raise important issues relating to the representation of immigrants that influence the micro-processes of immigration policy implementation in the two specific agencies in Florence, Italy. These findings show that the ethnicity of the immigrants is an important factor in the representation of immigrants in the receiving society's institutional structures. This is not manifested in "racial" terms, since such type of intolerance is considered morally wrong; instead, an ethnic stereotype is activated. The important issues are in fact revealed in a number of recurrent key words: the immigrant is a "foreigner" but not a "criminal", often "in need", and therefore s/he should be treated with "compassion" and at the same time should be taught the "Italian law and rules" by "professionals" who assist with "willingness" their "clients" regardless their "ethnic background".

Appendix

Table 1. Conditions for Issue of Entry Visa

X	subordinate employment (including artistic work)
X	freelance work
X	registration in employment lists
X	political asylum
X	Status as refugee
X	emigration
X	completion of paperwork for a job
X	Health
X	family
X	child adoption
X	child custody
X	visit to relatives
X	Study
X	judical proceedings
X	business
X	worship
X	special humanitarian causes (possibility of study and work permits)
X	tourism

Table 2. The Process and Related Administrative Agencies

Passport (or equivalent document)	Embassy (or Consulate)
Date of entry	Border controls
Regularization application receipt (if applicable)	*Questura*
Stay permit (original and copy)	*Questura*
Certificate of registration (if self-employment)	Commerce Chamber
Contract of employment (or employer's statement declaring specific time-period and fee of job to be undertaken (if dependent employment)	Employment Office
Employment booklet (for renewal)	Labor Inspection Office
Registration for tax authorities (for renewal)	Provincial Labor Office and Commerce Chamber
Residence registration	Municipality
Rent contract (or documents certifying suitable accommodation, i.e., accommodation meeting the minimum parameters as required by regional law)	Renting contract or Municipality

Table 3. Interview Themes

X	Task of the agency
X	Individual tasks of the agent – which task would you implement?
X	A typical example of their work
X	Co-operation with other agents (both form and content of cooperation)
X	With which immigrants they mostly deal
X	Legal documents – which sort of other guidance for the job?
X	Is there discretion – if yes, how is it exercised?
X	Effect for policy outcomes?
X	In your opinion, why do immigrants come to Italy?
X	In your opinion, who is considered an immigrant?
X	Describe the procedure followed at a typical case
X	Which cases are the most difficult/easy ones?
X	Organization: hierarchy
X	Resources: staff, workload, number of cases
X	Work pressure: long hours, shifts, stress; how do you cope with large workload and stress?
X	How do you feel in cases of sending off clients without having been serving them due to lack of resources or not meeting criteria for service/permission?

Table 4. Typified Expressions Used in the Daily Routine in the *Questura*

X	The officer in charge for this type of requests is on leave of absence today
X	I have just returned from leave of absence myself and I did not have the time to get informed about the case
X	Given that the office is very busy today, you may wish to return tomorrow instead
X	Say clearly your request; there are many people waiting for their turn
X	If you need to contact the director you may send him a fax at the office's central fax number
X	I have not seen today the director in the office. You may wish to call us tomorrow and you will be connected to the director's office.
X	The officer's line is busy at the moment, you may wish to leave your name and telephone number so that she/he can contact you when available.
X	I will come out (*of the counter*) and we will speak about this issue
X	Madam/Sir, the director wishes to speak to you inside, let me open the door for you.
X	I do not know *or* I really do not know
X	I know, I understand perfectly the particularity of your case, but what could I could; it is not me that handles this sort of request.
X	I do my job the best way I can
X	Do you have with you all the documents required for filling your application?
X	You should have read about the procedure in the note attached at the entrance
X	Let me see your passport before I can answer
X	"The foreigner" (*Lo straniero*)
X	Quiet, we are working for you
X	Sit down, please, wait for your turn

Endnotes

[1] This paper is based on the background study about Italy as a 'host' country, presented in the 2nd report (Veikou and Triandafyllidou, 2001) of an international project entitled "Does Implementation Matter" (IAPASIS), funded by the Fifth Framework Programme of the European Community. The project's aim was to examine immigration administration and control practices as well as the impact of organizational cultures and identity processes within institutional agencies on the implementation of ongoing policy in the field of immigration in four European countries. It included two northern European countries (Germany and the UK) and two southern European countries (Greece and Italy). During the years 2000–1, I conducted research on the Italian case, based at the Robert Schuman Centre for Advanced Studies, in Florence, Italy. The current paper is an outcome of this research.

[2] A full report on the analysis of the organizational culture and identity processes that influence the daily routines of "street–level bureaucrats" and the power relations between immigrants and employees within the institutional agencies involved in the immigration policy implementation in Florence, Italy, can be found in Veikou and Triandafyllidou 2001.

Works Cited

Brierley, W., and L. Giacometti. "Italian National Identity and the Failure of Regionalism." *Nation and Identity in Contemporary Europe*. Eds. B. Jenkins and S. Sofos. London: Routledge, 1996: 172-197.

Campani, G. "Immigration and Racism in Southern Europe: the Italian Case." *Ethnic and Racial Studies* 16:3 (1993): 507-555.

Cini, M. *The European Commission: Leadership, Organisation and Culture in the EU Administration*. Manchester: Manchester UP, 1996.

Cole, J. "Working Class Reactions to New Immigration in Palermo." *Critique of Anthropology* 16:2 (1996): 199-220.

---. *The New Racism in Europe: A Sicilian Ethnography*. Cambridge: Cambridge UP, 1997.

Collicelli, C. "Rome. City Template Regarding Element for Comparison." Report for the Project on Multicultural Policies and Modes of Citizenship in European Cities (UNESCO-MOST Programme) Rome Censis, June 1997.

Dente, B. *Governare la frammentazione: Stato Regioni ed enti locali in Italia.* Bologna: Il Mulino, 1985.

---. *Riformare la pubblica amministrazione: Italia Gran Bretagna Spagna Stati Uniti.* Torino: Fondazione Giovanni Agnelli, 1995.

Graziano, L., ed. *La crisi italiana* Torino: Einaudi, 1979.

Lewanski, R. "Italian Administration in Transition." *Southern European Society and Politics* 4:1 (1999): 97-131.

Quassoli, F., and M. Chiodi. Immigrazione e in/sicurezza in Emilia Romagna: Rappresentazioni sociali e pratiche organizzative di policia e magistratura. Project Report. Milan: December 2000.

Pasquino, G. *The End of Post-War Politics in Italy: the Landmark 1992 Elections.* Boulder: Westview Press, 1993.

Reyneri, E., et al. Migrant's Insertion in the Informal Economy. Deviant Behaviour and the Impact on Receiving Societies. The Comparative Reports. TSER Programme [unpublished project report], 1999.

Veikou, M., and A. Triandafyllidou. *Immigration Policy Implementation in Italy: Organisational Culture, Identity Processes and Labour Market Control.* 2nd Report IAPASIS Project [unpublished project report] RSCAS European University Institute, 2001.

---. "Immigration Policy and its Implementation in Italy – A Report on the State of the Art." *Migration Pathways. A Historic Demographic and Policy Review of Four Countries of the European Union.* Ed. A.Triandafyllidou. Brussels: European Commission Research Directorate, 2001.

Zincone, G. "Illegality Enlightenment and Ambiguity: A Hot Italian Recipe." *South European Society and Politics* 3:3 (1998): 43-82.

Contributors

Theron D. Cook is the President and Chief Executive Officer of Chasseur Group, an Alexandria, Virginia-based management consultant firm that focuses on providing strategic planning, program development and focused technical assistance to nonprofits and government. Prior to heading up Chasseur Group, Cook was the Senior Program Director of the Village Foundation where his portfolio included directing its multimillion dollar grantmaking department as well as directing its international affairs department that conducted various projects abroad. Before coming to the foundation, Cook was the National Vice President of Planning for MAD DADS, Inc., a Jacksonville, Florida-based national community mobilizing organization with 56 chapters in 16 states. MAD DADS has been awarded several Presidential and numerous national awards for its programmatic effectiveness and is widely considered an American best practice model. Cook presently sits on their Board of Directors. Cook is also the former Acting Director of the New York City Mayor's Office of Drug Abuse Policy where he directed their international affairs department conducting several projects at the United Nations. He is also the former Executive Director of the Paul Robeson Family Medical Center in New York City. A graduate of Harvard University and the Phillips Exeter Academy, Cook began his professional career as a foreign currency trader on Wall Street.

Maria I. Diedrich holds a Chair in American Studies and is director of the American Studies program at the University of Münster, Germany. Her work focuses on African American Studies, and she was the founding President of the Collegium for African American Research (CAAR) from 1992-2001. Since 1984, she has been a Fellow at the W.E.B. Du Bois Institute for Afro-American Research at Harvard University. Among her book publications are *Love Across Color Lines: Ottilie Assing and Frederick Douglass* (1999); *Ausbruch aus der Knechtschaft: Das amerikanische Slave Narrative* (1986); *Kommunismus im afroamerikanischen Roman* (1979); *The Black Columbiad* (ed. with Werner Sollors, 1994); *Black Imagination and the Middle Passage* (ed. with Henry Louis Gates, Jr., and Carl Pedersen, 1999); *Mapping African America* (ed. with Carl Pedersen and Justine Tally, 1999).

Contributors

Gerard Fergerson, PhD, is Director of Research, Planning, and Evaluation in the Executive Office of the Mayor/Office of the Deputy Mayor for Children, Youth, and Families in Washington, D.C. He oversees several health and social research and policy initiatives for the $2 billion health and human services cluster agencies. His research and policy interests include urban public health and public policy, disparities in health and social status, and child and youth development. In addition to his professional experience in senior public service positions, Gerard has held faculty appointments at New York University, Northwestern University, and Amherst College. His research and commentary has appeared in the *Journal of Urban Health*, *Journal of Adolescent Health*, and *Science as Culture*, among other publications. Dr. Fergerson holds a B.A. with high honors from Wesleyan University, M.A. in Afro-American Studies from Yale University, and PhD in the History of Science from Harvard University.

Jacob Gordon is Professor of African American Studies at the University of Kansas in Lawrence, Kansas as well as Executive Director of the Center for Multicultural Leadership. For more than thirty years, he has devoted much of his research to public policy issues, civil rights, education, substance abuse, the criminal justice system, and leadership. He has received and managed approximately $2.5 million in research and community service grants during his tenure at the University of Kansas. Among his scholarly works are 16 books, eight training manuals, ten monographs, ten chapters, 25 referred articles in academic journals, 15 research reports, numerous abstracts, and 74 papers and editorial works, including films.

Tamar Horowitz is a professor in the Department of Education at Ben-Gurion University and holds the Samuel and Miriam Hamburger Chair in Integration of Immigrant Communities. She has been conducting research since the 1970s on Russian and Ethiopian immigrants. She is the author of *Assimilation, Dialogue and Empowerment*, a book (in Hebrew) on the integration of Russian immigrants in a small town. She has written numerous articles on the integration of Russian immigrants and has edited four books on the subject: *The Soviet Man in an Open Society*; *Between Two Worlds: Children from the Soviet Union in Israel*, *Children of Perestroika in Israel*; and

Pacesetters and Losers (with Kotic and Hoffman). She was scholar in residence at the Ministry of Immigrant Absorption. Her current research is on hostility and violence among newcomers and longtime Israelis.

Ann Phoenix is a Senior Lecturer in Psychology at the Open University at Milton Keynes, England. She has previously worked at Birkbeck College, University of London, at Brunel University and at the Thomas Coram Research Unit, University of London, Institute of Education. Until October 2002 she was a Non-Executive Director on the Tavistock and Portman NHS Trust Board, on the Board of trustees of the National Family and Parenting Institute and on the Joseph Rowntree Foundation Children and Young People's Committee. She is a patron of the National Early Years Network. Her research interests include motherhood and the social identities of young people, particularly those associated with gender, "race", social class and adoption. Her publications include *Young Mothers?* (1991); *Black, White or Mixed Race? Race and Racism in the Lives of Young People of Mixed Parentage* (with B. Tizard, 1993; 2nd edition, 2002); *Shifting Identities Shifting Racisms* (ed. with Kum Kum Bhavnani, 1994); *Crossfires: Nationalism, Racism and Gender in Europe,* (ed. with Helma Lutz and Nira Yural-Davis, 1995); *New Dimensions in Midwifery Care* (with several co-authors, 1996); and *Young Masculinities* (with Stephen Frosh and Rob Pattman, 2002).

Nora Räthzel is Reader in Sociology at the University of Umeå, Sweden. Her research interests and publications include issues of ethnic and gender relations, racism, and spatial practices. She is currently investigating the access of young people of migrant and non-migrant background to the Swedish labor market and the usage of public space as a means to transgress ethnically segregated urban areas in Stockholm.

Birgit Rommelspacher, Dipl.Psych. Dr.phil. is Professor of Psychology, Gender and Ethnic Studies at the Alice Salomon Hochschule (University of Applied Scienes) Berlin. She also holds a teaching assignment (Privatdozentin) at the Technische Universität Berlin. In the past she was involved in research projects on institutional and family socialization and feminist psychology at the Deutsches Jugendinstitut in Munich. Also, she is a lecturer and researcher at the Freie University Berlin, focussing on networking in social services, professionalization and community health care. Among her publications are *Dominanzkultur* (1995), *Schuldlos-Schuldig? Wie sich junge Frauen mit Antisemitismus auseinandersetzen* (1995), und *Anerkennung und Ausgrenzung: Deutschland als multikulturelle Gesellschaft* (2002).

Ove Sernhede is a Researcher, Senior Lecturer and the head of the Departement for Cultural Studies at the University of Gothenburg, Sweden. He has published extensively in Swedish on African American music, youth cultures and theories on late modernity. Among his publications in English are *In Garageland. Youth, Rock and Modernity* (1996) and "Exoticism and Death as a Modern Taboo: Gangsta Rap and the Search for Intensity" in *Without Guarantees. In Honour of Stuart Hall* (Eds. Paul Gilroy, Lawrence Grossberg and Angela McRobbie, 2000).

Christiane Timmerman has a PhD in Social and Cultural Anthropology and coordinates the research on migration and ethnic minorities in the Research Group on Social Exclusion, Poverty and the City (OASeS) and in the Policy Research Centre on Equal Opportunities of the University of Antwerp. She teaches anthropology at the same university where she is also co-chair of the Antwerp Centre of Migration Studies. She was a visiting research fellow at the University of California, Berkeley.

Mariangela Veikou studied Social Anthropology at the London School of Economics and Political Science (UK) and obtained her PhD at the European University Institute (Italy). She held research positions at the European University Institute and the Robert Schumann Centre for Advanced Studies in Italy. She is currently a Marie Curie Research Fellow at the Institute for Migration and Ethnic Studies in the Netherlands. Her research interests are in theories on identity, ethnicity, migration and religion. In the field of methodology she has given particular attention to the links between fieldwork research, ethnography and the interpretation of oral sources. Her publications cover the areas of migration, ethnicity, religious diversity and ethnography.

Literatur: Forschung und Wissenschaft

Karl-Heinz Stoll
Die Interkulturalität afrikanischer Literatur
Chinua Achebe, Cyprian Ekwensi, Ngũgĩ wa Thiong'o, Wole Soyinka
Die englische Sprache in Afrika, die literarischen Medien Roman und Drama sowie die Themen der afrikanischen Literatur sind Ausdruck kultureller Pluralität. Der Beitrag postkolonialer Literatur zu unserem Orientierungswissen besteht in ihrem Potenzial sprachlicher und inhaltlicher Desorientierung als Voraussetzung einer Emanzipation von eurozentrischen Vorurteilen. Das Buch geht ein auf die englische Sprache als Medium wirtschaftlicher Globalisierung und kultureller Fragmentarisierung. Dann werden anhand der Eigenarten von Sprache, Handlungsführung, Introspektionen und mythologischem Ideengehalt die Werke der vier bedeutendsten schwarzafrikanischen Autoren exemplarisch als „Dazwischen-Literatur" interpretiert.
Zielgruppe sind Anglisten, Afrikanisten und alle, die sich für die Rolle von Kultur in unserer globalisierten Welt interessieren.
Bd. 1, 2003, 400 S., 30,90 €, br., ISBN 3-8258-6698-x

FORECAAST
(Forum for European Contributions to African American Studies)

Maria Diedrich; Carl Pedersen; Justine Tally (eds.)
Mapping African America
History, Narrative Formation, and the Production of Knowledge
The world of African America extends throughout the northern, central, southern and insular parts of the American continent. The essays included in this volume take the creation of that world as a single object of study, tracing significant routes and contacts, building comparisons and contrasts. They thus participate in the reworking of traditional approaches to the study of history, the critique of literature and culture, and the production of knowledge. All are engaged in an effort to locate the African American experience within a wider pan-African vision that links the colonial with the postcolonial, the past with the present, the African with the Western.
Mapping African America sketches lines that, far from limiting our geography, extend our knowledge of the Africanist influence on and their participation in what is generally called "Western" culture. This creative challenge to traditional disciplines will not only enhance the reader's understanding of African American Studies but will also help forge links with other academic fields of inquiry.
Bd. 1, 1999, 256 S., 30,90 €, br., ISBN 3-8258-3328-3

Stefanie Sievers
Liberating Narratives
The Authorization of Black Female Voices in African American Women Writers' Novels of Slavery
Three contemporary novels of slavery – Margaret Walker's *Jubilee* (1966), Sherley Anne Williams's *Dessa Rose* (1986) and Toni Morrison's *Beloved* (1987) – are the central focus of *Liberating Narratives*. In significantly different ways that reflect their individual and socio-political contexts of origin, these three novels can all be read as critiques of historical representation and as alternative spaces for remembrance – 'sites of memory' – that attempt to shift the conceptual ground on which our knowledge of the past is based.
Bd. 2, 1999, 232 S., 25,90 €, br., ISBN 3-8258-3919-2

Justine Tally
Paradise Reconsidered
Toni Morrison's (Hi)stories and Truths
Toni Morison's *Paradise* (1998) arrived on the scene amid vociferous acclaim and much consternation. Third in the trilogy begun with *Beloved* and *Jazz*, this fascinating yet complicated the novel has sown as much confusion as admiration. How does it work? How does the novel close the trilogy? Indeed, a major complaint among reviewers, why does Morrison overload us with so many characters and stories? In this first book-length study of *Paradise*, Justin Tally securely links the work to Morrison's entire oeuvre and effectively argues that while all of the novels of the trilogy are deeply analytical of the relationship of memory, story and history, the historical narrative: memory is fickle, story is unreliable, and history is subject to manipulation. A master narrative of the past is again dictated by the dominant discourse, but this time the control exerted is black und male, not white and male. Though this stranglehold threatens to deaden life and put the future on hold, Morrison's narrative disruptions challenge the very nature of this "paradise" on earth.
Bd. 3, 1999, 112 S., 17,90 €, br., ISBN 3-8258-4204-5

LIT Verlag Münster – Hamburg – Berlin – London
Grevener Str./Fresnostr. 2 48159 Münster
Tel.: 0251 – 23 50 91 – Fax: 0251 – 23 19 72
e-Mail: vertrieb@lit-verlag.de – http://www.lit-verlag.de

Dorothea Fischer-Hornung; Alison D. Goeller (eds.)
EmBODYing Liberation
The Black Body in American Dance
A collection of essays concerning the black body in American dance, *EmBODYing Liberation* serves as an important contribution to the growing field of scholarship in African American dance, in particular the strategies used by individual artists to contest and liberate racialized stagings of the black body. The collection features special essays by Thomas DeFrantz and Brenda Dixon Gottschild, as well as an interview with Isaac Julien.
Bd. 4, 2001, 152 S., 20,90 €, br., ISBN 3-8258-4473-0

Patrick B. Miller; Therese Frey Steffen; Elisabeth Schäfer-Wünsche (eds.)
The Civil Rights Movement Revisited
Critical Perspectives on the Struggle for Racial Equality in the United States
The crusade for civil rights was a defining episode of 20th century U.S. history, reshaping the constitutional, political, social, and economic life of the nation. This collection of original essays by both European and American scholars includes close analyses of literature and film, historical studies of significant themes and events from the turn-of-the century to the movement years, and assessments of the movement's legacies. Ultimately, the articles help examine the ways civil rights activism, often grounded in the political work of women, has shaped American consciousness and culture until the outset of the 21st century.
Bd. 5, 2001, 224 S., 24,90 €, br., ISBN 3-8258-4486-2

Fritz Gysin; Christopher Mulvey (Eds.)
Black Liberation in the Americas
The recognition that Africans in the Americas have also been subjects of their destiny rather than merely passive objects of European oppression represents one of the major shifts in twentieth-century mainstream historiography. Yet even in the eighteenth and nineteenth centuries, slave narratives and abolitionist tracts offered testimony to various ways in which Africans struggled against slavery, from outright revolt to day-to-day resistance. In the first decades of the twentieth century, African American historians like Carter G. Woodson and W. E. B. Du Bois started to articulate a vision of African American history that emphasized survival and resistance rather than victimization and oppression. This volume seeks to address these and other issues in black liberation from interdisciplinary and comparative perspectives, focusing on such issues as slave revolts, day-to-day resistance, abolitionist movements, maroon societies, the historiography of resistance, the literature of resistance, black liberation movements in the twentieth century, and black liberation and post colonial theory. The chapters span the disciplines of history, literature, anthropology, folklore, film, music, architecture, and art, drawing on the black experience of liberation in the United States, the Caribbean, and Latin America.
Bd. 6, 2001, 280 S, 24,90 €, br., ISBN 3-8258-5137-0

Justine Tally
The Story of *Jazz*
Toni Morrison's Dialogic Imagination
Ever since its publication in 1992, *Jazz*, probably Toni Morrison's most difficult novel to date, has elicited a wide array of critical response. Many of these analyses, while both thoughtful and thought-provoking, have provided only partial or inherently inconclusive interpretations. The title, and certain of the author's own pronouncements, have led other critics to focus on the music itself, both as medium and aesthetic support for the narration.
Bd. 7, 2001, 168 S., 20,90 €, br., ISBN 3-8258-5364-0

Mar Gallego
Passing Novels in the Harlem Renaissance
Identity Politics and Textual Strategies
Passing Novels in the Harlem Renaissance offers an insightful study of the significance of passing novels for the literary and intellectual debate of the Harlem Renaissance. Mar Gallego effectively uncovers the presence of a subversive component in five of these novels (by James Weldon Johnson, George Schuyler, Nella Larsen, and Jessie Fauset, turning them into useful tools to explore the passing phenomenon in all its richness and complexity. Her compelling study intends to contribute to the ongoing revision of the parameters conventionally employed to analyze passing novels by drawing attention to a great variety of textual strategies such as double consciousness, parody, and multiple generic covers. Examining the hybrid nature of these texts, Gallego skillfully highlights their radical critique of the status quo and their celebration of a distinct African American identity.
"*Passing Novels in the Harlem Renaissance* is an impressive work of scholarship and interpretation. It is well researched and stimulating to read."
Hanna Wallinger, University of Salzburg
"Mar Gallego draws our renewed attention to the uses and subversions of the trope of passing that have characterized the African American novelistic tradition also in the twentieth century."
Giulia Fabi, University of Ferrara

LIT Verlag Münster – Hamburg – Berlin – London
Grevener Str./Fresnostr. 2 48159 Münster
Tel.: 0251 – 23 50 91 – Fax: 0251 – 23 19 72
e-Mail: vertrieb@lit-verlag.de – http://www.lit-verlag.de

"Mar Gallego's thorough scholarship now provides us with a new, in-depth and refreshing reading of texts we thought we already knew something about. A provocative text and a welcome addition to the field!" Justine Tally, University of La Laguna
Bd. 8, 2003, 224 S., 24,90 €, br., ISBN 3-8258-5842-1

Paola Boi; Sabine Broeck (Eds.)
CrossRoutes – The Meanings of "Race" for the 21st Century
This collection reflects the still urgent project of historical recuperation, as well as an examination of literary representations and other cultural manifestations of the Black Diaspora. Disciplinary work within the boundaries of African American Studies has been enhanced by more general considerations of the history of rr-aceänd racism in globalized contexts. The articles assembled here reflect recent empirical research as well as challenging theoretical considerations. Contributions address particular formations of racialized modernity owed to the impact of the Atlantic slave trade and slavery, and thus broaden the approach to the Middle Passage, to improve our understanding of it as a constitutive transatlantic phenomenon in the widest possible sense.
Bd. 9, 2003, 272 S., 25,90 €, br., ISBN 3-8258-6651-3

Sylvia Mayer (ed.)
Restoring the Connection to the Natural World
Essays on the African American Environmental Imagination
Since its emergence in the second half of the nineteenth century American environmentalism had predominantly been a white, middle-class pursuit, preoccupied with notions of wilderness and wildlife preservation. Only fairly recently, with the advent of the environmental justice movement in the 1980s, has American environmentalism broadened its definition of "environment" to include the concerns relevant to a community's way of living. Especially the concerns of poor urban communities of color, which have been exposed to environmental hazards disproportionately, have entered the political agenda. This volume - one of the first collections of ecocritical essays devoted exclusively to African American texts - shows that African Americans have contributed to the efforts of the environmental justice movement not only as political activists, but also as writers. The essays range from studies of nineteenth-century slave narratives to twentieth-century texts by Zora Neale Hurston, Claude McKay, Richard Wright, Charles Johnson, Toni Cade Bambara, Audre Lorde, and Octavia Butler. Employing a variety of theoretical and methodological premises, they provide insight into the texts' various conceptualizations of "nature," "culture," and "humanness" and their implications for environmental ethics.
Bd. 10, 2003, 208 S., 20,90 €, br., ISBN 3-8258-6732-3

Kimberley Phillips; Hermine Pinson; Lorenzo Thomas; Hanna Wallinger (eds.)
Critical Voicings of Black Liberation
Resistance and Representations in the Americas
The contributions to "Critical Voices of Black Liberation in the Americas" originated from the 1999 CAAR Conference in Münster and from conferences held in the US in 2000 and 2001. More than half of the eleven essays consider black performances on stage, in sound, and on film; the remaining essays explore slavery, African American literature, and nineteenth-century black educators. These exciting essays creatively examine artistic and/or political articulation of black liberation as the construction of a new critical and signifyin(g) voice. This liberated and critical voice asserts itself as much as a communal expression of black subjectivities as it is an articulation of the black self.
Bd. 11, 2003, 192 S., 20,90 €, br., ISBN 3-8258-6739-0

Ana María Manzanas; Jesús Benito
Intercultural Mediations
Hybridity and Mimesis in American Literatures
Intercultural Mediations proposes a study of the multiple crossings between and among the different literary traditions of the United States. The volume draws upon two main theoretical sources, namely postcolonial theory and American Border Studies, and aims to articulate a model of the hybrid, postcolonial and liminal nature of writing in the US. Ana Mª Manzanas and Jesús Benito explore the nature of the ëthnicÖthers' appropriation, dialogization and Subversion of the Euroamerican authoritative discourse – embodied in what the authors call the Book of the West – as well as the inscription of cultural difference on the white page. Their analysis focuses on the production of contestatory sites of enunciation in a few particular fields and texts from the literatures of the US, such as John Milton Oskison's The Problem of Old Harjo,Toni Morrison's Beloved, Helena Viramontes's The Cariboo Café,Carlos Fuentes's La frontera de crystal, Ron Arias's The Road to Tamazunchale, Frederick Douglass's Narrative, Louise Erdrich's Tracks, José Barreiro's

The Indian Chronicles, and Caryl Phillip's Crossing the River. The authors use a comparative approach which underscores the aesthetic and epistemic ruptures that ethnic and marginalized wridng is producing on Western culture's general text, in order to open up new sites of enunciation and new spaces for the hybridizaäon of traditional hegemonic discourses.
Bd. 12, 2003, 224 S., 25,90 €, br., ISBN 3-8258-6738-2

American Studies in Austria
edited by Prof. Dr. Astrid Fellner (University of Vienna), Prof. Dr. Klaus Rieser (University of Graz), Prof. Dr. Hanna Wallinger (University of Salzburg)

Heinz Tschachler; Maureen Devine; Michael Draxlbauer (Eds.)
The EmBodyment of American Culture
American culture has literally become fixated on the body at the same time that the body has emerged as a key term within critical and cultural theory. Contributions thus address the body as a site of the cultural construction of various identities, which are themselves enacted, negotiated, or subverted through bodily practices. Contributions come from literary and cultural studies, film and media studies, history and sociology, and women studies, and are representative of many theoretical positions, hermeneutic, historical, structuralist, feminist, postmodernist. They deal with representations and discursifications of the body in a broad array of texts, in literature, the visual arts, theater, the performing arts, film and mass media, science and technology, as well as in various cultural practices.
Bd. 1, 2003, 224 S., 19,90 €, br., ISBN 3-8258-6762-5

"Human Potentialities"
Studien zu Aldous Huxley & zeitgenössischer Kultur
Studies in Aldous Huxley & Contemporary Culture
herausgegeben von / edited by
Prof. Dr. Bernfried Nugel (Universität Münster)
und Prof. Dr. Lothar Fietz (Universität Tübingen)

Gerhard Wagner
The 'Beauty-Truths' of Literature
Elemente einer Dichtungstheorie in Aldous Huxleys Essayistik
Aldous Huxley hat zwar keine systematische Literaturästhetik verfaßt, doch spielen dichtungstheoretische Fragestellungen in seinem umfangreichen essayistischen Werk eine ausgesprochen wichtige Rolle. Seine Überlegungen zum Sinn und Zweck sowie zu den Grenzen und Möglichkeiten der Literatur sind fester Bestandteil seines philosophischen Denkens und geprägt von seiner Auffassung der besonderen Erfahrungs- und Ausdrucksfähigkeiten des wahren Dichters. Für ihn ist höhere Dichtung Träger von Erkenntnis, nämlich in Form von "beauty-truths".
Die vorliegende Studie analysiert und systematisiert Huxleys literarthcoretische Vorstellungen und gelangt dabei zu einem heuristischen Denkmodell, das weit ausführlicher und kohärenter ist, als bislang angenommen wurde. Idealziel der Dichtung ist demnach ein Gesamtentwurf, der die unmittelbar-gefühlsmäßige Erlebenswelt des Menschen wie auch sein rational-wissenschaftliches Denken und darüber hinaus die Welt des aus menschlicher Perspektive Nebensächlichen und Unbedeutenden erfaßt. Indem die Untersuchung Huxleys graduelle Wendung von einer betont skeptischen hin zu einer mystischen Weltperspektive berücksichtigt, gibt sie außerdem Aufschluß über Konstanten und Entwicklungen seines dichtungstheoretischen Denkens.
Bd. 3, 2001, 280 S., 30,90 €, br., ISBN 3-8258-5358-6

Evelyn Firchow; Bernfried Nugel (eds)
Reluctant Modernists: Aldous Huxley and Some Contemporaries
A Collection of Essays by Peter Edgerly Firchow. With an Introduction by Jerome Meckier and a Personal Memoir by Janice Rossen. Presented on the Occasion of his 65th Birthday December 16, 2002
The essays collected here deal with modernist writers who, on the whole, felt 'reluctant' about their modernist status because they believed that it was just as important to look backward as it

was to look forward. Indeed, for most of them looking backward was more important because it was only through the past that one could understand one's proper place in the present and in the future. That is why in Huxley's *Brave New World* it is the rejection of the past in the future – and by implication in the present – that makes its satire so penetrating. Modernism, in other words, means for these writers not a radical break with the past but a continuing search for what still connects them (and us) vitally with it.
Bd. 4, 2003, 352 S., 30,90 €, br., ISBN 3-8258-5962-2

Hallenser Studien zur Anglistik und Amerikanistik

hrsg. am Institut für Anglistik und Amerikanistik (Universität Halle-Wittenberg)

Angela Kuhk
Vielstimmige Welt
Die Werke St. John de Crèvecœurs in deutscher Sprache
"Das Werk hat unter den Händen des Teutschen Übersetzers noch gewonnen." Die europaweite Begeisterung für die Werke Crèvecœurs äußerte sich auch in einer Flut an deutschen Übersetzungen: Zwischen 1782 und 1802 entstanden mehr als 30 Schriften, die auf die Zeilen des berühmten "Amerikanischen Landmanns" zurückgingen.
Erstmals erfolgt hier eine bibliographische Erfassung und eine chronologische Vorstellung dieser Texte wie auch der Rezeptionsdokumente.
Ausführliche Übersetzungsanalysen zu den Themen Indianer, Quäker, Sklaverei, deutsche Einwanderer, Walfang, Flora und Fauna liefern neue Beiträge zum deutschen Amerikabild im ausgehenden 18. Jahrhundert und erlauben einen detaillierten Einblick in die vielstimmige Welt Crèvecœurs.
Bd. 8, 2001, 480 S., 25,90 €, br., ISBN 3-8258-4882-5

Wolf Kindermann;
Gisela Hermann-Brennecke (eds.)
Echoes in a Mirror: The English Institute after 125 Years
This volume is published in honor of the 125th anniversary of the English Institute at the Martin-Luther University in Halle-Wittenberg, one of the earliest of its kind in Germany. Its long tradition of research in historical linguistics had a considerable impact on literary, cultural and educational studies. Many of the scholars who taught and researched here over the past 125 years tried to uphold academic standards, scholarly values, and personal integrity even in turbulent times of ideological pressure and political turmoil.
Even now, 12 years after the wall came down, the process of restructuring that it triggered has not come to an end. In spite of this, faculty and staff are standing their ground by linking up with the legacy handed down to them.
This volume presents current research at the Institute in a collection of essays on *Beowulf*, "Elizabethan Parliaments", "Black Vernacular English", "Denotational Incongruencies", "Newspaper English", "Interrogating Whiteness", Edgar Allan Poe, Charlotte Lennox, T. S. Eliot, Salman Rushdie, David Lodge, and on empirical issues related to foreign language acquisition research and to teacher training programs.
Bd. 9, 2001, 264 S., 20,90 €, br., ISBN 3-8258-5675-5

Andreas Marschollek
Kognitive und affektive Flexibilität durch fremde Sprachen
Eine empirische Untersuchung in der Primarstufe
Inwieweit Kinder Fremdem offen begegnen und ihre Persönlichkeit weiter entwickeln, hängt wesentlich von ihrem Zugang zu fremden Sprachen ab. Der vorliegende Band untersucht – theoretisch und empirisch – den Beitrag, den ein Unterricht mit fremden Sprachen in der Primarstufe dazu leisten kann.
Die Ergebnisse legen es nahe, Schülerinnen und Schüler immer wieder gezielt an eine bewusste Auseinandersetzung mit Sprache(n), Identität und Einstellungen heranzuführen.
Ein entsprechendes vom Autor entwickeltes und in der Praxis erprobtes Unterrichtskonzept wird vorgestellt und kritisch analysiert.
Bd. 10, 2002, 320 S., 24,90 €, br., ISBN 3-8258-6262-3